PENGUIN PLAYS

TINY ALICE, BOX and QUOTATIONS FROM CHAIRMAN MAO TSE-TUNG

Edward Albee, the American dramatist, was born in 1928. His plays include *The Zoo Story* (1958), *The Death of Bessie Smith* (1959), *The Sandbox* (1959), *The American Dream* (1960), a stage adaptation of Carson McCullers's novel *The Ballad of the Sad Café* (1963), *Tiny Alice* (1964) and *Malcolm* (1965). In 1967 he was awarded the Pulitzer Prize for *A Delicate Balance*. In the same year he wrote *Everything in the Garden* (after a play by Giles Cooper), and in the following year two one-act plays, *Box* and *Quotations from Chairman Mao Tse-tung*. His latest play, *All Over*, will be published in the autumn of 1972.

D1334764

TINY ALICE, BOX
and
QUOTATIONS FROM
CHAIRMAN MAO TSE-TUNG

EDWARD ALBEE

PENGUIN BOOKS

Penguin Books Ltd, Harmondsworth, Middlesex, England
Penguin Books Australia Ltd, Ringwood, Victoria, Australia

—

Tiny Alice first published in Great Britain by
Jonathan Cape 1966
Published in Penguin Books 1971
Copyright © Edward Albee, 1965

Box and *Quotations from Chairman Mao Tse-Tung* first
published in Great Britain by Jonathan Cape 1970
Published in Penguin Books 1971
Copyright © Edward Albee, 1968, 1969

—

Made and printed in Great Britain
by Richard Clay (The Chaucer Press) Ltd,
Bungay, Suffolk
Set in Monotype Baskerville

—

TINY ALICE

For Noel Farrand

AUTHOR'S NOTE

It has been the expressed hope of many that I would write a preface to the published text of *Tiny Alice*, clarifying obscure points in the play – explaining my intention, in other words. I have decided against creating such a guide because I find – after reading the play over – that I share the view of even more people: that the play is quite clear. I will confess, though, that *Tiny Alice* is less opaque in reading than it would be in any single viewing. One further note: this printed text of *Tiny Alice* represents the complete play. Some deletions – mainly in the final act – were made for the New York production; and while I made the deletions myself, and quite cheerfully, realizing their wisdom in the particular situation, I restore them here with even greater enthusiasm.

EDWARD ALBEE

First performed at the Billy Rose Theatre, New York City,
29 December 1964

LAWYER	*William Hutt*
CARDINAL	*Eric Berry*
JULIAN	*John Gielgud*
BUTLER	*John Heffernan*
MISS ALICE	*Irene Worth*

Directed by ALAN SCHNEIDER

Sets by WILLIAM RITMAN
Gowns by MAINBOCHER
Lighting by MARTIN ARONSTEIN

ACT ONE

Scene One

The CARDINAL's *garden. What is needed . . . ? Ivy climbing a partial wall of huge stones? An iron gate? Certainly two chairs — one, the larger, obviously for His Eminence ; the other, smaller — and certainly an elaborate birdcage, to stage left, with some foliage in it, and two birds, cardinals . . . which need not be real.*

> *[At rise, the* LAWYER *is at the birdcage, talking to the birds.]*

LAWYER: Oomm, yoom, yoom, um? Tick-tick-tick-tick-tick. Um? You do-do-do-do-do-um? Tick-tick-tick-tick-tick-tick-tick-um? *[He raises his fingers to the bars.]* Do-do-do-do-do-do-do? Aaaaaawwwww! Oomm, yoom, yoom, um?

> *[The* CARDINAL *enters from stage right — through the iron gates? — unseen by the* LAWYER, *who repeats some of the above as the* CARDINAL *moves toward centre.]*

CARDINAL *[finally. Quietly amused]*: Saint Francis?

LAWYER *[swinging around; flustered; perhaps more annoyed than embarrassed at being discovered]*: Your Eminence!

CARDINAL: Our dear Saint Francis, who wandered in the fields and forests, talked to all the . . .

LAWYER *[moving to kiss the ring]*: Your Eminence, we appreciate your kindness in taking the time to see us; we know how heavy a schedule you . . .

CARDINAL *[silencing him by waving his ring at him. The* LAWYER *kneels, kisses the ring, rises]*: We are pleased . . . *we* are pleased to be your servant *[Trailing off.]* . . . if . . . we can be your servant. We addressed you as Saint Francis . . .

LAWYER *[properly mumbling]*: Oh, but surely . . .

CARDINAL: ... as Saint Francis ... who did talk to the birds so, did he not. And here we find *you*, who talk not only to the birds but to [*with a wave at the cage*] – you must forgive us – to cardinals as well. [*Waits for reaction, gets none, tries again.*] ... To cardinals? As well?

LAWYER [*a tight smile*]: We ... we understood.

CARDINAL [*he, too*]: Did we.

> [*A brief silence, as both smiles hold.*]

LAWYER [*to break it, moving back toward the cage*]: We find it droll – if altogether appropriate in this setting – that there should be two cardinals ... uh, together ... [*Almost a sneer.*] ... in conversation, as it were.

CARDINAL [*the smile again*]: Ah, well, they are a comfort to each other ... companionship. And they have so much to say. They ... understand each other so much better than they would ... uh, *other* birds.

LAWYER: Indeed. And so much better than they would understand saints?

CARDINAL [*daring him to repeat it, but still amused*]: Sir?

LAWYER [*right in*]: That cardinals understand each *other* better than they understand saints.

CARDINAL [*not rising to it*]: Who is to say? Will you sit?

LAWYER [*peering into the cage*]: They are extraordinary birds ... cardinals, if I may say so. ...

CARDINAL [*through with it*]: You push it too far, sir. Will you join us?

> [*He moves to his chair, sits in it.*]

LAWYER [*brief pause, then surrender; moves to the other chair*]: Of course.

CARDINAL [*a deep sigh*]: Well. What should we do now? [*Pause.*] Should we clap our hands [*Does so, twice.*] ... twice, and have a monk appear? A very old monk? With just a ring of white hair around the base of his head, stooped, fast-shuffling, his hands deep in his sleeves? Eh? And should we send him for wine? Um? Should we offer

you wine, and should we send him scurrying off after it?
Yes? Is that the scene you expect now?

LAWYER [*very relaxed, but pointed*]: It's so difficult to know
what to expect in a Cardinal's garden, Your Eminence.
An old monk would do . . . or – who is to say? – perhaps
some good-looking young novice, all freshly scrubbed,
with big working-class hands, who would . . .

CARDINAL [*magnanimous*]: We have both in our service; if
a boy is more to your pleasure . . .

LAWYER: I don't drink in the afternoon, so there is need
for neither . . . unless Your Eminence . . . ?

CARDINAL [*his eyes sparkling with the joke to come about his
nature*]: We are known to be . . . ascetic, so we will have
none of it. Just . . . three cardinals . . . and Saint Francis.

LAWYER: Oh, not Saint Francis, not a saint. Closer to a
king; closer to Croesus. That was gibberish I was speaking
to the cardinals – and it's certainly not accepted that
Saint Francis spoke gibberish to his . . . parishioners . . .
intentional gibberish or otherwise.

CARDINAL: It is not accepted; no.

LAWYER: No. May I smoke?

CARDINAL: Do.

LAWYER [*lights up*]: Closer to Croesus; to gold; closer to
wealth.

CARDINAL [*a heavy, weary sigh*]: Aahhhh, you *do* want to
talk business, don't you?

LAWYER [*surprisingly tough*]: Oh, come on, Your Eminence:
[*softer*] do you want to spend the afternoon with me,
making small talk? Shall we . . . shall we talk about . . .
times gone by?

CARDINAL [*thinks about it with some distaste*]: No. No no;
we don't think so. It wouldn't do. It's not charitable of
us to say so, but when we were at school we did loathe you
so.

[*Both laugh slightly.*]

LAWYER: Your Eminence was not . . . beloved of everyone himself.

CARDINAL [*thinking back, a bit smugly*]: Ah, no; a bit out of place; out of step.

LAWYER: A swine, I thought.

CARDINAL: And we you.

[*Both laugh a little again.*]

LAWYER: Do you ever slip?

CARDINAL: Sir?

LAWYER: Mightn't you – if you're not careful – [*tiny pause*] lapse . . . and say *I* to me . . . not we?

CARDINAL [*pretending sudden understanding*]: Ah *ha*! Yes, we under*stand*.

LAWYER: Do we, do we.

CARDINAL: We do. We – and here we speak of our*selves* and not of our station – we . . . *we* reserve the first-person singular for intimates . . . and equals.

LAWYER: . . . And your superiors.

CARDINAL [*brushing away a gnat*]: The case does not apply.

LAWYER [*matter-of-factly; the vengeance is underneath*]: You'll grovel, Buddy. [*Slaps his hip hard.*] As automatically and naturally as people slobber on that ring of yours. As naturally as that, I'll have you do your obeisance. [*Sweetly.*] As you used to, old friend.

CARDINAL: We . . . [*Thinks better of what he was about to say.*] You *were* a swine at school. [*More matter-of-factly.*] A cheat in your examinations, a liar in all things of any matter, vile in your personal habits – unwashed and indecent, a bully to those you could intimidate and a sycophant to everyone else. We remember you more clearly each moment. It is law you practise, is it not? We find it fitting.

LAWYER [*a mock bow, head only*]: We are of the same school, Your Eminence.

CARDINAL: And in the same class . . . but not *of*. You have come far – in a worldly sense . . . from so little, we mean. [*Musing.*] The law.

LAWYER: I speak plainly.

CARDINAL: You are plain. As from your beginnings.

LAWYER [*quietly*]: Overstuffed, arrogant, pompous son of a profiteer. And a whore. You are in the Church, are you not? We find it fitting.

CARDINAL [*a burst of appreciative laughter*]: You're *good!* You *are! Still!* Gutter, but good. But, in law . . . [*Leaves it unfinished with a gesture.*] Ah! It comes back to us; it begins to. What did we call you at school? What name, what nickname did we have for you . . . all of us? What term of simple honesty and . . . rough affection did we have for you? [*Tapping his head impatiently.*] It comes back to us.

LAWYER [*almost a snarl*]: We had a name for you, too.

CARDINAL [*dismissing it*]: Yes, yes, but we forget it.

LAWYER: Your Eminence was not always so . . . eminent.

CARDINAL [*remembering*]: Hy-e . . . [*relishing each syllable*] Hy-e-na. Hy. E. Na. We recall.

LAWYER [*close to break-through anger*]: We are close to Croesus, Your Eminence. I've brought gold with me . . . [*leans forward*] money, Your Eminence.

CARDINAL [*brushing it off*]: Yes, yes; later. Hy-e-na.

LAWYER [*a threat, but quiet*]: A great deal of money, Your Eminence.

CARDINAL: We hear you, and we will discuss your business shortly. And why did we call you hyena . . .?

LAWYER [*quiet threat again*]: If Croesus goes, he takes the gold away.

CARDINAL [*outgoing*]: But, Hyena, you are not Croesus; you are Croesus' emissary. You will wait; the gold will wait.

LAWYER: Are you certain?

CARDINAL [*ignoring the last*]: Ah, yes, it was in natural-science class, was it not? [*The* LAWYER *rises, moves away a little.*] Was it not?

LAWYER: Considering your mother's vagaries, you were never certain of your true father ... were you?

CARDINAL: Correct, my child: considering one's mother's vagaries, one was never certain of one's true father ... was one? But then, my child, we embraced the Church; and we *know* our true father. [*Pause; the* LAWYER *is silent.*] It was in natural-science class, eleven-five until noon, and did we not discover about the hyena ...

LAWYER: More money than you've ever seen!

CARDINAL [*parody; cool*]: Yum-yum. [*Back to former tone.*] Did we not discover about the hyena that it was a most resourceful scavenger? That, failing all other food, it would dine on offal ...

LAWYER [*angrier*]: Millions!

CARDINAL [*pressing on*]: ... and that it devoured the wounded and the dead? We found that last the most shocking: the dead. But we were young. And what horrified us most – and, indeed, what gave us all the thought that the name was most fitting for yourself –

LAWYER [*ibid.*]: Money!

CARDINAL: ... was that to devour its dead, scavenged prey, it would often chew into it ...

LAWYER: MONEY, YOU SWINE!

CARDINAL [*each word rising in pitch and volume*]: ... chew into it THROUGH THE ANUS????
    [*Both silent, breathing a little hard.*]

LAWYER [*finally; softly*]: Bastard.

CARDINAL [*quietly, too*]: And now that we have brought the past to mind, and remembered what we could not exactly, shall we ... talk business?

LAWYER [*softly; sadly*]: Robes the colour of your mother's vice.

CARDINAL [*kindly*]: Come. Let us talk business. You are a businessman.

LAWYER [*sadly again*]: As are you.

CARDINAL [*as if reminding a child of something*]: We are a Prince of the Church. Do you forget?

LAWYER [*suddenly pointing to the cage; too offhand*]: Are those two lovers? Do they mate?

CARDINAL [*patronizing; through with games*]: Come; let us talk business.

LAWYER [*persisting*]: Is it true? Do they? Even cardinals?

CARDINAL [*a command*]: If you have money to give us . . . sit down and give it.

LAWYER: To the lay mind – to the cognoscenti it may be fact, accepted and put out of the head – but to the lay mind it's speculation . . . voyeuristic, perhaps, and certainly anti-Rome . . . mere speculation, but whispered about, even by the school children – indeed, as you must recall, the more . . . urbane of us wondered about the Fathers at school . . .

CARDINAL: . . . the more wicked . . .

LAWYER: . . . about their vaunted celibacy . . . among one another. Of course, we were at an age when everyone diddled everyone else . . .

CARDINAL: Some.

LAWYER: Yes, and I suppose it was natural enough for us to assume that the priests did too.

CARDINAL [*as if changing the subject*]: You have . . . fallen away from the Church.

LAWYER: And into the arms of reason.

CARDINAL [*almost thinking of something else*]: An unsanctified union: not a marriage: a whore's bed.

LAWYER: A common-law marriage, for I am at law and, as you say, common. But it is quite respectable these days.

CARDINAL [*tough; bored with the church play-acting; heavy and tired*]: All right; that's enough. What's your business?

LAWYER [*pacing a little, after an appreciative smile*]: My employer . . . wants to give some of her money to the Church.

CARDINAL [*enthusiastic, but guarded*]: Does she!

LAWYER: Gradually.

CARDINAL [*understanding*]: *Ah*-ha.

LAWYER [*offhand*]: A hundred million now.

CARDINAL [*no shown surprise*]: And the rest gradually.

LAWYER: And the same amount each year for the next twenty – a hundred million a year. She is not ill; she has no intention of dying; she is quite young, youngish; there is no . . . rush.

CARDINAL: Indeed not.

LAWYER: It is that she is . . . overburdened with wealth.

CARDINAL: And it weighs on her soul.

LAWYER: Her soul is in excellent repair. If it were not, I doubt she'd be making the gesture. It is, as I said, that she is overburdened with wealth, and it . . . uh . . .

CARDINAL [*finding the words for him*]: . . . piles up.

LAWYER [*a small smile*]: . . . and it is . . . wasted . . . lying about. It is one of several bequests – arrangements – she is making at the moment.

CARDINAL [*not astonishment, but unconcealed curiosity*]: One of several?

LAWYER: Yes. The Protestants as well, the Jews . . . hospitals, universities, orchestras, revolutions here and there . . .

CARDINAL: Well, we think it is a . . . responsible action. She is well, as you say.

LAWYER: Oh, yes; very.

CARDINAL: We are . . . glad. [*Amused fascination.*] How did you become her . . . lawyer, if we're not intruding upon . . .?

LAWYER [*brief pause; tight smile*]: She had a dossier on me, I suppose.

CARDINAL: It must be a great deal less revealing than ours . . . than our dossier on you.

LAWYER: Or a great deal *more* revealing.

CARDINAL: For her sake, and yours, we hope so.

LAWYER: To answer your question: I am a very good lawyer. It is as simple as that.

CARDINAL [*speculating on it*]: You *have* escaped prison.

LAWYER: I've done nothing to be imprisoned for.

CARDINAL: Pure. You're pure. You're ringed by stench, but you're pure. There's an odour that precedes you, and follows after you're gone, but you walk in the eye of it . . . pure.

LAWYER [*contemptuous*]: Look, pig, I don't enjoy you.

CARDINAL [*mockingly; his arms wide as if for an embrace*]: School chum!

LAWYER: If it were not my job to . . .

CARDINAL [*abruptly*]: Well, it is! Do it!

LAWYER [*a smile to a hated but respected adversary*]: I've given you the facts: a hundred million a year for twenty years.

CARDINAL: But . . .?

LAWYER [*shrugs*]: That's all.

CARDINAL [*stuttering with quiet excitement*]: Y-y-y-y-yes, b-b-but shall I just go to the *house* and pick it up in a *truck*?

LAWYER [*great, heavy relief*]: AAAAAAHHHHHHHHHHHHHHH.

CARDINAL [*caught up short*]: Hm? [*No reply.*] HM???

LAWYER: Say it again. Say it once again for me.

CARDINAL [*puzzled; suspicious*]: What? Say what?

LAWYER [*leaning over him*]: Say it again; repeat what you said. It was a sweet sound.

CARDINAL [*shouting*]: SAY WHAT!

LAWYER [*cooing into his ear*]: 'Yes, but shall I just go to the house and pick it up in a truck?'

CARDINAL [*thinks on it a moment*]: Well, perhaps there was a bit . . . perhaps there was too much levity there . . . uh, if one did not know one . . .

LAWYER [*coos again*]: . . . 'But shall *I* just go to the house . . .'

CARDINAL: Wh . . . NO!

LAWYER [*sings it out*]: Shall IIIIIII just go!

CARDINAL [*cross*]: No! We . . . we did not say that!

LAWYER: IIIIIIIIIIIIII.

CARDINAL [*a threat*]: We did not say 'I'.

LAWYER [*almost baby talk*]: We said I. Yes, we did; we said I. [*Suddenly loud and tough.*] We said I, and we said it straight. I! I! I! By God, we picked up our skirts and lunged for it! IIIIIII! Me! Me! Gimme!

CARDINAL [*full shout*]: WE SAID NO SUCH THING!

LAWYER [*oily imitation*]: We reserve the first-person singular, do we not, for . . . for intimates, equals . . . or superiors. [*Harsher.*] Well, my dear, you found all three applying. Intimate. How close would we rub to someone for all that wealth? As close as we once did?

CARDINAL [*not wanting to hear, but weak*]: Leave . . . leave off.

LAWYER [*pressing*]: Equals? Oh, money equals anything you want. Levels! LEVELS THE EARTH! AND THE HEAVENS!

CARDINAL: ENOUGH!!

LAWYER [*the final thrust*]: . . . Or superiors. Who is superior, the one who stands on the mount of heaven? We think not! We have come down off our plural . . . when the stakes are high enough . . . and the hand, the kissed hand palsies out . . . FOR THE LOOT!!

CARDINAL [*hissed*]: Satan!

LAWYER [*after a pause*]: Satan? You would believe it . . . if you believed in God. [*Breaks into – for lack of a better word – Satanic laughter, subsides. Patronizing now.*] No, poor Eminence, you don't have to drive a truck around to the back door for it. We'll get the money to you . . . to your . . . people. Fact, I don't want you coming 'round . . . at all. Clacketing through the great corridors of the place, sizing it up, not content with enough wealth to buy off the first two hundred saints picked out of a bag, but wondering if *it* mightn't get thrown into the bargain as a . . . summer residence, perhaps . . . uh, after she dies and scoots up to heaven.

CARDINAL [*on his feet, but shaky, uncertain*]: This . . . uh . . .

LAWYER: . . . interview is terminated?

CARDINAL [*quietly*]: This is unseemly talk.

LAWYER [*vastly, wryly amused*]: Oh? Is it?

CARDINAL [*a mechanical toy breaking down*]: We will . . . we will forgive your presumption, your . . . excess . . . ex*cuse*, yes . . . excuse? . . . We will . . . overlook your . . . [*A plea is underneath.*] Let us have no more of this talk. It *is* unseemly.

LAWYER [*businesslike; as if the preceding speech had not happened*]: As I said, I don't want you coming 'round . . . bothering her.

CARDINAL [*humble*]: I would not bother the lady; I have not met her. Of course, I would very much like to have the pleasure of . . .

LAWYER: We slip often now, don't we.

CARDINAL [*very soul-weary*]: Pardon?

LAWYER: The plural is gone out of us, I see.

CARDINAL: Ah. Well. Perhaps.

LAWYER: Regird yourself. We *are* about terminated. [*Quick, insulting finger-snaps.*] Come! Come! Back up; back on your majesty! Hup!

CARDINAL [*slowly, wearily coming back into shape*]: Uh . . . yes . . . of – of course. We, uh, we shall make any arrangements you wish . . . naturally. We . . . we have no desire to intrude ourselves upon . . . uh . . . upon . . .

LAWYER: Miss Alice.

CARDINAL: Yes; upon Miss Alice. If she . . . if Miss Alice desires privacy, certainly her generosity has earned it for her. We . . . would not intrude.

LAWYER: You *are* kind. [*Fishing in a pocket for a notebook.*]

What . . . is . . . your . . . secretary's . . . name . . . I think I have it . . . right . . . [*Finds notebook.*]

CARDINAL: Brother . . . .

LAWYER: Julian! Is that not right?

CARDINAL: Yes, Brother Julian. He is an old friend of ours; we . . .

LAWYER: Rather daring of you, wasn't it? Choosing a lay brother as your private secretary?

CARDINAL [*a combination of apology and defiance*]: He is an old friend of ours, and he has served the . . .

LAWYER [*praising a puppy*]: You are adventurous, are you not?

CARDINAL: He has been assigned many years to the . . .

LAWYER [*waving his notebook a little*]: We have it; all down; we know.

CARDINAL [*a little sadly*]: Ah-ha.

LAWYER: Yes. Well, we will send for your . . . Brother Julian. . . . To clear up odds and ends. Every bank has its runners. We don't ask vice presidents to . . . fetch and carry. Inform Your Brother Julian. We will send for him.

    [LAWYER *exits.*]

CARDINAL [*to the exiting figure*] Yes, we . . . will. [*Stands still, looks at the ground, tired, looks at his sleeves, his fingernails, his ring, up, out, over. Sighs, looks at the cage. Smiles slightly, moves to the cage, the fingers of his left hand fluttering at it.*] Do . . . do you . . . do you have much to say to one another, my dears? Do you? You find it comforting? Hmmmmm? Do you? Hmmmm? Do-do-do-do-do-do-do-do? Hmmmmmm? Do?

CURTAIN

Scene Two

*The library of a mansion – a castle. Pillared walls, floor-to-ceiling
leather-bound books. A great arched doorway, rear centre. A huge
reading table to stage left – practical. A phrenological head on it.
To stage right, jutting out of the wings, a huge doll's-house model
of the building of which the present room is a part. It is as tall as a
man, and a good deal of it must be visible from all parts of the
audience. An alternative – and perhaps more practical – would be
for the arched doorway to be either left or right, with bookshelves
to both sides of the set, coming toward the centre, and to have the
entire doll's house in the rear wall, in which case it could be smaller
– say, twelve feet long and proportionately high. At any rate, it is
essential.*

    [*At rise,* JULIAN *is alone on stage, looking at the house.*]

JULIAN [*after a few moments of head-shaking concentration*]:
    Extraordinary . . . extraordinary.

BUTLER [*after entering, observing* JULIAN, *not having heard
    him*]: Extraordinary, isn't it?

JULIAN [*mildly startled*]: Uh . . . yes, unbelievable . . . [*Agree-
    ing.*] Extraordinary.

BUTLER [*who moves about with a kind of unbutlerlike ease*]: I
    never cease to wonder at the . . . the fact of it, I
    suppose.

JULIAN: The workmanship . . .

BUTLER [*a mild correction*]: That someone would do it.

JULIAN [*seeing*]: Yes, yes.

BUTLER: That someone would . . . well, for heaven's sake,
    that someone would build . . . [*refers to the set*] . . . *this*
    . . . castle? . . . and then . . . duplicate it in such precise

miniature, so exactly. Have you looked through the windows?

JULIAN: No, I . . .

BUTLER: It is exact. Look and see.

JULIAN [*moves even closer to the model, peers through a tiny window*]: Why . . . why, YES. I . . . there's a great . . . baronial dining room, even with tiny candlesticks on the tables!

BUTLER [*nodding his head, a thumb back over his shoulder*]: It's down the hall, off the hallway to the right.

JULIAN [*the proper words won't come*]: It's . . . it's . . .

BUTLER: Look over here. There; right there.

JULIAN [*peers*]: It's . . . it's this *room*! This room we're *in*!

BUTLER: Yes.

JULIAN: Extraordinary.

BUTLER: Is there anyone there? Are we there?

JULIAN [*briefly startled, then laughs, looks back into the model*]: Uh . . . no. It seems to be quite . . . empty.

BUTLER [*a quiet smile*]: One feels one should see one's self . . . almost.

JULIAN [*looks back to him; after a brief, thoughtful pause*]: Yes. That would be rather a shock, wouldn't it?

BUTLER: Did you notice . . . did you notice that there is a model within that room in the castle? A model of the model?

JULIAN: I . . . I did. But . . . I didn't register it, it seemed so . . . continual.

BUTLER [*a shy smile*]: You don't suppose that within that tiny model in the model there, there is . . . another room like this, with yet a tinier model within it, and within . . .

JULIAN [*laughs*]: . . . and within and within and within and . . .? No, I . . . rather doubt it. It's remarkable craftsmanship, though. Remarkable.

BUTLER: Hell to clean.

JULIAN [*conversational enthusiasm*]: Yes! I should think so! Does it open from . . .

BUTLER: It's sealed. Tight. There is no dust.

JULIAN [*disappointed at being joked with*]: Oh.

BUTLER: I was sporting.

JULIAN: Oh.

BUTLER [*straight curiosity*]: Did you mind?

JULIAN [*too free*]: I! No!

BUTLER [*doctrine, no sarcasm*]: It would almost be taken for granted – one would think – that if a person or a person's surrogate went to the trouble, *and* expense, of having such a dream toy made, that the person *would* have it sealed, so that there'd be no dust. Wouldn't one think.

JULIAN [*sarcasm and embarrassment together*]: One would think.

BUTLER [*after a pause, some rue*]: I have enough to do as it is.

JULIAN [*eager to move on to something else*]: Yes, yes!

BUTLER: It's enormous . . . [*A sudden thought.*] even for a castle, I suppose. [*Points to the model.*] Not that. [*Now to the room.*] This.

JULIAN: Endless! You . . . certainly you don't work alone.

BUTLER: Oh, Christ, no.

JULIAN [*reaffirming*]: I would have *thought*.

BUTLER [*almost daring him to disagree*]: Still, there's enough work.

JULIAN [*slightly testy*]: I'm *sure*.

[*A pause between them.*]

BUTLER [*for no reason, a sort of 'Oh, what the hell'*]: Heigh-ho.

JULIAN: Will there be . . . someone? . . . to see me? . . . soon?

BUTLER: Hm?

JULIAN: Will there be someone to see me soon! [*After a blank stare from the other.*] You announced me? I trust?

BUTLER [*snapping to*]: Oh! Yes! [*Laughs.*] Sorry. Uh . . . yes, there will be someone to see you soon.

JULIAN [*attempt at good-fellowship*]: Ah, good!

BUTLER: Are you a priest?

JULIAN [*self-demeaning*]: I? No, no . . .

BUTLER: If not Catholic, Episcopal.

JULIAN: No . . .

BUTLER: What, then?

JULIAN: I am a lay brother. I am not ordained.

BUTLER: You are *of* the cloth but have not taken it.

JULIAN [*none too happy*]: You *could* say that.

BUTLER [*no trifling*]: One *could* say it, and quite accurately.
   May I get you some ice water?

JULIAN [*put off and confused*]: No!

BUTLER [*feigns apology*]: Sorry.

JULIAN: You must forgive me. [*Almost childlike enthusiasm.*]
   This is rather a big day for me.

BUTLER [*nods understandingly*]: Iced *tea*.

JULIAN [*laughs*]: No . . . nothing, thank you . . . uh . . . I
   don't have your name.

BUTLER: Fortunate.

JULIAN: No, I meant that . . .

BUTLER: Butler.

JULIAN: Pardon?

BUTLER: Butler.

JULIAN: Yes. You . . . you *are* the butler, are you not,
   but . . .

BUTLER: Butler. My name is Butler.

JULIAN [*innocent pleasure*]: How extraordinary!

BUTLER [*putting it aside*]: No, not really. Appropriate:
   Butler . . . butler. If my name were Carpenter, and I
   were a butler . . . or if I *were* a carpenter, and my name
   were Butler . . .

JULIAN: But *still* . . .

BUTLER: . . . it would not be so appropriate. And think:
   if I were a woman, and had become a chambermaid, say,
   and my name were Butler . . .

JULIAN [*anticipating*]: . . . you would be in for some rather tiresome exchanges.

BUTLER [*cutting, but light*]: None more than this.

JULIAN [*sadly*]: Aha.

BUTLER [*forgiving*]: Coffee, then.

JULIAN [*as if he can't explain*]: No. Nothing.

BUTLER [*semi-serious bow*]: I am at your service.
   [LAWYER *enters.*]

LAWYER: I, too.

JULIAN: Ah!

LAWYER: I'm sorry to have kept you waiting, but . . .

JULIAN: Oh, no, no . . .

LAWYER: . . . I was conferring with Miss Alice.

JULIAN: Yes.

LAWYER [*to* BUTLER; *no fondness*]: Dearest.

BUTLER [*to* LAWYER; *same*]: Darling.

LAWYER [*to* JULIAN]: Doubtless, though, you two have . . .
   [*Waves a hand about.*]

JULIAN: Oh, we've had a most . . . unusual . . .

LAWYER [*to* BUTLER, *ignoring* JULIAN'*s answer*]: You've offered our guest refreshments?

JULIAN: Brother Julian.

BUTLER: Ice water, iced tea, and coffee – hot assumed, I imagine – none taken.

LAWYER: Gracious! [*Back to* JULIAN.] Port, perhaps. Removed people take port, I've noticed.

JULIAN [*more to please than anything*]: Yes. Port. Please.

LAWYER [*to* BUTLER]: Port for . . .

JULIAN: Julian – Brother Julian.

LAWYER [*slightly patronizing*]: I *know*. [BUTLER *goes to a sideboard.*] I would join you, but it is not my habit to drink before sundown. Not a condemnation, you understand. One of my minor disciplines.

BUTLER [*generally, looking at the bottle*]: The port is eighteen-oh-six. [*To the* LAWYER.] How do they fortify wines, again?

JULIAN: Alcohol is added, more alcohol ... at the time of casking. Fortify ... strengthen.

BUTLER: Ah, yes.

LAWYER [*to* JULIAN]: Of course, your grandfather was a vintner, was he not.

JULIAN: Goodness, you ... you have my history.

LAWYER: Oh, we do. Such a mild life ... save those six years in your thirties which are ... blank ... in our report on you.

JULIAN [*a good covering laugh*]: Oh, they were ... mild, in their own way. Blank, but not black.

LAWYER: Will you fill them for us? The blank years?

JULIAN [*taking the glass from* BUTLER]: Thank you. [*The laugh again.*] They were nothing.

LAWYER [*steelier*]: Still, you will fill them for us.

JULIAN [*pleasant, but very firm*]: No.

BUTLER: Gracious!

LAWYER: Recalcitrance, yes ... well, we must have our people dig further.

JULIAN: You'll find nothing interesting. You'll find some ... upheaval, but ... waste, mostly. Dull waste.

LAWYER: The look of most of our vices in retrospect, eh?

BUTLER [*light*]: I have fleshpot visions: carousals, thighs and heavy perfume. ...

LAWYER [*to* BUTLER]: It's in your mind, fitting, a mind worthy of your name. [*To* JULIAN.] Did you two ... did he tell you his name, and did you two have a veritable badminton over it? Puns and chuckles?

JULIAN: We ... laboured it a bit, I more than ... Butler, it would appear.

BUTLER: I was churlish, I'm sorry. If there weren't so many of *you* and only one of *me* ...

JULIAN: Oh, now ...

LAWYER [*still on it*]: You're not going to tell me about those six years, eh?

JULIAN [*stares at him for a moment, then says it clearly, enunciating*]: No.

    [LAWYER *shrugs.*]

BUTLER: May I have some port?

LAWYER [*slightly incredulous*]: Do you *like* port?

BUTLER: Not very, but I thought I'd keep him company while you play police.

LAWYER [*shrugs again*]: It's not my house. [*Turns to* JULIAN.] One can't say, 'It's not my castle,' can one? [*Back to* BUTLER.] If you think it's proper.

BUTLER [*getting himself some*]: Well, with the wine cellar stacked like a munitions dump, and you 'never having any' until the barn swallows start screeping around . . .

LAWYER: There's no such word as screep.

BUTLER [*shrugs*]: Fit.

JULIAN: I think it has a nice onomatopoeic ring about it . . .

LAWYER [*down to business, rather rudely*]: Your buddy told you why we sent for you?

JULIAN [*offended, but pretending confusion*]: My . . . buddy?

LAWYER: Mine, really. We were at school together. Did he tell you that? [*As* JULIAN *intentionally looks blank.*] His Eminence.

JULIAN: Ah!

LAWYER [*imitation*]: Ah! [*Snapped.*] Well? Did he?

JULIAN [*choosing his words carefully, precisely*]: His Eminence informed me . . . generally. He called me into his . . .

LAWYER: . . . garden . . .

JULIAN: . . . garden . . . which is a comfortable office in summer . . .

BUTLER: Ninety-six today.

JULIAN [*interested*]: Indeed!

BUTLER: More tomorrow.

LAWYER [*impatiently*]: Called you into his garden.

JULIAN: And – sorry – and . . . told me of the high honour
which he had chosen for me.

LAWYER [*scoffing*]: He. Chosen. You.

JULIAN: Of . . . your lady's most . . .

LAWYER: Miss Alice.

JULIAN: Of Miss Alice's – sorry, I've not met the lady yet,
and first names – of her overwhelming bequest to the
Church . . .

LAWYER: Not a bequest; a bequest is made in a will; Miss
Alice is not dead.

JULIAN: Uh . . . grant?

LAWYER: Grant.

JULIAN [*taking a deep breath*]: Of her overwhelming grant
to the Church, and of my assignment to come here, to
take care of . . .

LAWYER: Odds and ends.

JULIAN [*shrugs one shoulder*]: . . . if you like. 'A few questions
and answers' was how it was put to me.

BUTLER [*to* LAWYER, *impressed*]: He's a lay brother.

LAWYER [*bored*]: We *know*. [*For* JULIAN's *benefit*.] His
Eminence – buddy . . .

JULIAN [*natural, sincere*]: Tch–tch–tch–tch–tch . . .

LAWYER: He was my buddy at school . . . if you don't
mind. [*Beginning, now, to* BUTLER, *but quickly becoming
general*.] His Eminence – though you have never met him,
Butler, seen him, perhaps – is a most . . . eminent man;
and bold, very bold; behind – or, underneath – what
would seem to be a solid rock of . . . pomposity, sham,
peacocking, there is a . . . flows a secret river . . . of . . .

BUTLER [*for* JULIAN's *benefit*]: This is an endless metaphor.

LAWYER: . . . of unconventionality, defiance, even. Simple
sentences? Is that all you want? Did you know that
Brother Julian here is the only lay brother in the history
of Christendom assigned, chosen, as secretary and con-
fidant to a Prince of the Church? Ever?

JULIAN [*mildly*]: That is not known as fact.

LAWYER: Name others!

JULIAN: I say it is not known as fact. I grant it is not usual
– my appointment as secretary to His Eminence. . . .

LAWYER [*faint disgust*]: An honour, at any rate, an unusual
honour for a lay brother, an honour accorded by a most
unusual Prince of the Church – a prince of a man, in
fact – a prince whose still waters . . . well, you finish it.

BUTLER [*pretending puzzlement as to how to finish it*]: . . . whose
still waters . . .

JULIAN: His Eminence is, indeed, a most unusual man.

LAWYER [*sourly*]: I said he was a prince.

BUTLER [*pretending to be talking to himself*]: . . . run quiet?
Run deep? Run *deep*! *That's* good!

LAWYER: Weren't there a few eyebrows raised at your
appointment?

JULIAN: There . . . I was not informed of it . . . if there
were. His Eminence would not burden me. . . .

LAWYER [*still to* JULIAN, *patronizing*]: He is really Santa
Claus; we know.

JULIAN [*rising to it*]: Your animosity toward his Eminence
must make your task very difficult for you. I must say
I . . .

LAWYER: I have learned . . . [*Brief pause before he says the
name with some distaste.*] Brother Julian . . . never to con-
fuse the representative of a . . . thing with the thing itself.

BUTLER: . . . though I wonder if you'd intended to get
involved in *two* watery metaphors there: underground
river, and still waters.

LAWYER [*to* BUTLER]: No, I had not. [*Back to* JULIAN.] A
thing with its representative. Your Cardinal and I loathe
one another, and I find him unworthy of contempt. [*A
hand up to stop any coming objection.*] A cynic and a hypocrite,
a posturer, but all the same the representative of an august
and revered . . . body.

JULIAN [*murmured*]: You are most unjust.

LAWYER [*as if he were continuing a prepared speech*]: Uh . . . revered body. And Rome, in its perhaps wily – though *cer*tainly inscrutable – wisdom, Rome has found reason to appoint that wreckage as its representative.

JULIAN: Really, I can't permit you to talk that way.

LAWYER: You will permit it, you're under instructions, you have a job to do. In fact, you have this present job be*cause* I cannot stand your Cardinal.

JULIAN: He . . . he did not tell me so.

LAWYER: *We* tell you so. [JULIAN *dips his head to one side in a 'perhaps it is true' gesture.*] And it is so.

JULIAN: I will not . . . I will not concern myself with . . . all this.

BUTLER [*quite to himself*]: I don't *like* port.

LAWYER [*to* BUTLER]: Then don't drink it. [*To* JULIAN.] You're quite right: bow your head, stop up your ears and do what you're told.

JULIAN: Obedience is not a fault.

LAWYER: Nor always a virtue. See Fascism.

JULIAN [*rather strong for him*]: Perhaps we can get on with our business. . . .

LAWYER [*he, too*]: You don't want to take up my time, or your own.

JULIAN: Yes.

BUTLER [*putting down glass*]: Then I won't drink it.

LAWYER [*to* JULIAN, *briskly, as to a servant*]: All right! I shall tell Miss Alice you've come – that the drab fledgling is pecking away in the library, impatient for . . . food for the Church.

JULIAN [*a tight smile, a tiny formal bow*]: If you would be so kind.

LAWYER [*twisting the knife*]: I'll find out if she cares to see you today.

JULIAN [*ibid.*]: Please.

LAWYER [*moving toward the archway*]: And, if she cares to, I will have you brought up.

JULIAN [*mild surprise, but not a question*]: Up.

LAWYER [*almost challenging him*]: Up. [*Pause.*] You will not tell us about the six years – those years blank but not black . . . the waste, the dull waste.

JULIAN [*small smile*]: No.

LAWYER [*he, too*]: You will . . . in time. [*To* BUTLER.] Won't he, Butler? Time? The great revealer?

      [LAWYER *exits.*]

JULIAN [*after the* LAWYER *is gone; no indignation*]: Well.

BUTLER [*offhand*]: Nasty man.

JULIAN [*intentionally feigning surprise*]: Oh? [HE *and* BUTLER *laugh.*] Up.

BUTLER: Sir?

JULIAN: Up.

BUTLER: Oh! Yes! She . . . [*Moves to the model.*] has her apartments up . . . here. [*He points to a tower area.*] Here.

JULIAN: A-ha.

BUTLER [*straightening things up*]: About those six years . . .

JULIAN [*not unfriendly, very matter-of-fact*]: What of them?

BUTLER: Yes, what of them?

JULIAN: Oh . . . [*Pause.*] I . . . I lost my faith. [*Pause.*] In God.

BUTLER: Ah. [*Then a questioning look.*]

JULIAN: Is there more?

BUTLER: *Is* there more?

JULIAN: Well, nothing . . . of matter. I . . . declined. I . . . shrivelled into myself; a glass dome . . . descended, and it seemed I was out of reach, unreachable, finally unreaching, in this . . . paralysis, of sorts. I . . . put myself in a mental home.

BUTLER [*curiously noncommittal*]: Ah.

JULIAN: I could not reconcile myself to the chasm between the nature of God and the use to which men put . . . God.

BUTLER: Between your God and others', your view and theirs.

JULIAN: I said what I intended: [*weighs the opposites in each hand*] it is God the mover, not God the puppet; God the creator, not the God created by man.

BUTLER [*almost pitying*]: Six years in the loony bin for semantics?

JULIAN [*slightly flustered, heat*]: It is not semantics! Men create a false God in their own image, it is easier for them! . . . It is not . . .

BUTLER: Levity! Forget it!

JULIAN: I . . . yes.

[*A chime sounds.*]

BUTLER: Miss Alice will see you. I will take you up.

JULIAN: Forgive me . . . I . . .

BUTLER [*moves toward archway*]: Let me show you up.

JULIAN: You *did* ask me.

BUTLER [*level*]: Yes, and you told me.

JULIAN [*an explanation, not an apology*]: My faith and my sanity . . . they are one and the same.

BUTLER: Yes? [*Considers it.*] A-ha. [*Smiles noncommittally.*] We must not keep the lady waiting.

[*They begin exiting,* BUTLER *preceding* JULIAN.]

CURTAIN

Scene Three

An upstairs sitting room of the castle. Feminine, but not frilly. Blues instead of pinks. Fireplace in keeping with the castle. A door to the bedroom in the rear wall, stage left; a door from the hallway in the side wall, stage left.

> [*At rise,* MISS ALICE *is seated in a wing chair, facing windows, its back to the audience; the* LAWYER *is to one side, facing her.*]

LAWYER [*pause, he has finished one sentence, is pondering another*]: . . . Nor is it as simple as all that. The instinct of giving may die out in our time – if you'll grant that giving is an instinct. The government is far more interested in taking, in regulated taking, than in promoting spontaneous generosity. Remember what I told you – what we discussed – in reference to the charitable foundations, and how . . . [*A knock on the hall door.*] That will be our bird of prey. Pray. P-R-A-Y. What a pun I could make on that; bird of pray. Come in.

> [*The hall door opens;* BUTLER *precedes* JULIAN *into the room.*]

BUTLER: Brother Julian, who *was* in the library, is now here.

LAWYER: So he is. [*To* JULIAN, *impatiently.*] Come in, come in.

JULIAN [*advancing a little*]: Yes . . . certainly.

BUTLER: May I go? I'm tired.

LAWYER [*grandly*]: By all means.

BUTLER [*turns to go*]: Thank you. [*To* JULIAN.] Goodbye.

JULIAN: Goodb . . . I'll . . . we'll see one another again?

BUTLER: Oh. Yes, probably. [*As he exits.*] Goodbye, everybody.

LAWYER [*after* BUTLER *exits, chuckles*]: What is it the
nouveaux riches are always saying? 'You can't get good
servants nowadays'?

JULIAN: He seems . . .

LAWYER [*curt*]: He is very good. [*Turns to the chair.*] Miss
Alice, our Brother Julian is here. [*Repeats it, louder.*] OUR
BROTHER JULIAN IS HERE. [*To* JULIAN.] She's terribly
hard of hearing. [*To* MISS ALICE.] DO YOU WANT TO
SEE HIM? [*To* JULIAN.] I think she's responding.
Sometimes . . . well, at her age and condition . . . twenty
minutes can go by . . . for her to assimilate a sentence and
reply to it.

JULIAN: But I thought . . . His Eminence said she was . . .
young.

LAWYER: SHHHHHHHH! She's moving.

[MISS ALICE *slowly rises from her chair and comes around
it. Her face is that of a withered crone, her hair grey and white
and matted; she is bent; she moves with two canes.*]

MISS ALICE [*finally, with a cracked and ancient voice, to* JULIAN]:
Hello there, young man.

LAWYER [*as* JULIAN *takes a step forward*]: Hah! Don't come
too close, you'll unnerve her.

JULIAN: But I'm terribly puzzled. I was led to believe that
she was a young woman, and . . .

MISS ALICE: Hello there, young man.

LAWYER: Speak to her.

JULIAN: Miss . . . Miss Alice, how do you do?

LAWYER: Louder.

JULIAN: HOW DO YOU DO?

MISS ALICE [*to* LAWYER]: How do I do *what*?

LAWYER: It's a formality.

MISS ALICE: WHAT!?

LAWYER: IT IS A FORMALITY, AN OPENING GAMBIT.

MISS ALICE: Oh. [*To* JULIAN.] How do *you* do?

JULIAN: Very well . . . thank you.

MISS ALICE: WHAT!?

JULIAN: VERY WELL, THANK YOU.

MISS ALICE: Don't you scream at me!

JULIAN [*mumbled*]: Sorry.

MISS ALICE: WHAT!?

JULIAN: SORRY!

MISS ALICE [*almost a pout*]: Oh.

LAWYER [*who has enjoyed this*]: Well, I think I'll leave you two now . . . for your business. I'm sure you'll have a . . .

JULIAN [*an attempted urgent aside to the* LAWYER]: Do you think you . . . shouldn't you be here? You've . . . you've had more experience with her, and . . .

LAWYER [*laughing*]: No, no, you'll get along fine. [*To* MISS ALICE.] I'LL LEAVE YOU TWO TOGETHER NOW. [MISS ALICE *nods vigorously*.] HIS NAME IS BROTHER JULIAN, AND THERE ARE SIX YEARS MISSING FROM HIS LIFE. [*She nods again.*] I'LL BE DOWNSTAIRS. [*Begins to leave.*]

MISS ALICE [*when the* LAWYER *is at the door*]: Don't steal anything.

LAWYER [*exiting*]: ALL RIGHT!

JULIAN [*after a pause, begins bravely, taking a step forward*]: Perhaps you should sit down. Let me . . .

MISS ALICE: WHAT!?

JULIAN: PERHAPS YOU SHOULD SIT DOWN!

MISS ALICE [*not fear; malevolence*]: Keep away from me!

JULIAN: Sorry. [*To himself.*] Oh, really, this is impossible.

MISS ALICE: WHAT!?

JULIAN: I SAID THIS WAS IMPOSSIBLE.

MISS ALICE [*thinks about that for a moment, then*]: If you're a defrocked priest, what're you doing in all that? [*Pointing to* JULIAN'S *garb.*]

JULIAN: I AM NOT A DEFROCKED PRIEST, I AM A LAY BROTHER. I HAVE NEVER BEEN A PRIEST.

MISS ALICE: What did you drink downstairs?

JULIAN: I had a glass of port ... PORT!

MISS ALICE [*a spoiled, crafty child*]: You didn't bring *me* one.

JULIAN: I had no idea you ...

MISS ALICE: WHAT!?

JULIAN: SHALL I GET YOU A GLASS?

MISS ALICE: A glass of *what*.

JULIAN: PORT. A GLASS OF PORT.

MISS ALICE [*as if he were crazy*]: What for?

JULIAN: BECAUSE YOU ... [*To himself again.*] Really, this *won't* do.

MISS ALICE [*straightening up, ridding herself of the canes, assuming a normal voice*]: I agree with you, it won't do, really.

JULIAN [*astonishment*]: I beg your pardon?

MISS ALICE: I said it won't do at all. [*She unfastens and removes her wig, unties and takes off her mask, becomes herself, as* JULIAN *watches, openmouthed.*] There. Is that better? And you needn't yell at me any more; if anything, my hearing is *too* good.

JULIAN [*slightly put out*]: I ... I don't understand.

MISS ALICE: Are you annoyed?

JULIAN: I suspect I will be ... might be ... after the surprise leaves me.

MISS ALICE [*smiling*]: Don't be; it's only a little game.

JULIAN: Yes, doubtless. But why?

MISS ALICE: Oh, indulge us, please.

JULIAN: Well, of course, it would be my pleasure ... but, considering the importance of our meeting ...

MISS ALICE: Exactly. Considering the importance of our meeting.

JULIAN: A ... a test for me.

MISS ALICE [*laughs*]: No, not at all, a little lightness to counter the weight. [*Mock seriousness.*] For we are involved in weighty matters . . . the transfer of millions, the rocking of empires. [*Normal, light tone again.*] Let's be comfortable, shall we? Swing my chair around.

  [JULIAN *moves to do so.*]

As you can see – you *can*, I trust – I'm *not* a hundred and thirteen years old, but I *do* have my crotchets, even now: I have chairs everywhere that are mine – in each room . . . a chair that is mine, that I alone use.

JULIAN [*moving the chair*]: Where would you . . .

MISS ALICE [*lightly*]: Just . . . swing it . . . around. You needn't move it. Good. Now, sit with me. [*They sit.*] Fine. In the dining room, of course, there is no question – I sit at the head of the table. But, in the drawing rooms, or the library, or whatever room you wish to mention, I have a chair that I consider my possession.

JULIAN: But you possess the entire . . . [*thinks of a word*] establishment.

MISS ALICE: Of course, but it is such a large . . . establishment that one needs the feel of specific possession in every . . . area.

JULIAN [*rather shy, but pleasant*]: Do you become . . . cross if someone accidentally assumes your chair, one of your chairs?

MISS ALICE [*thinks about it, then*]: How odd! Curiously, it has never happened, so I cannot say. Tell me about yourself.

JULIAN: Well, there isn't much to say . . . much that isn't already known. Your lawyer would seem to have assembled a case book on me, and . . .

MISS ALICE: Yes, yes, but not the things that would interest him, the things that would interest me.

JULIAN [*genuine interest*]: And what are they?

MISS ALICE [*laughs again*]: Let me see. Ah! Do I terrify you?

JULIAN: You *did*, and you are still . . . awesome.

MISS ALICE [*sweetly*]: Thank you. Did my lawyer intimidate you?

JULIAN: It would seem to be his nature – or his pleasure – to intimidate, and . . . well, I am, perhaps, more easily intimidated than some.

MISS ALICE: Perhaps you are, but he *is* a professional. And how did you find Butler?

JULIAN: A gentle man, quick . . . but mostly gentle.

MISS ALICE: Gentle, yes. He was my lover at one time. [*As JULIAN averts his head.*] Oh! Perhaps I shouldn't have told you.

JULIAN: No, forgive me. Things sometimes . . . are so unexpected.

MISS ALICE: Yes, they are. I am presently mistress to my lawyer – the gentleman who intimidated you so. He is a pig.

JULIAN [*embarrassed*]: Yes, yes. You have . . . never married.

MISS ALICE [*quiet amusement*]: Alas.

JULIAN: You are . . . not Catholic.

MISS ALICE [*the same*]: Again, alas.

JULIAN: No, it is fortunate you are not.

MISS ALICE: I am bored with my present lover.

JULIAN: I . . . [*Shrugs.*]

MISS ALICE: I was not soliciting advice.

JULIAN [*quiet laugh*]: Good, for I have none.

MISS ALICE: These six years of yours.

JULIAN [*says it all in one deep breath*]: There is no mystery to it, my faith in God left me, and I committed myself to an asylum. [*Pause.*] You see? Nothing to it.

MISS ALICE: What an odd place to go to look for one's faith.

JULIAN: You misunderstand me. I did not go there to *look* for my faith, but because *it* had left me.

MISS ALICE: You tell it so easily.

JULIAN [*shrugs*]: It is easy to tell.

MISS ALICE: Ah.

JULIAN [*giggles a little*]: However, I would not tell your present . . . uh, your lawyer. And that made him quite angry.

MISS ALICE: Have you slept with many women?

JULIAN [*carefully*]: I am not certain.

MISS ALICE [*Tiny laugh.*]: It is an easy enough thing to determine.

JULIAN: Not so. For one, I am celibate. A lay brother – you must know – while not a priest, while not ordained, is still required to take vows. And chastity is one of them.

MISS ALICE: A dedicated gesture, to be sure, celibacy without priesthood . . . but a melancholy one, for you're a handsome man . . . in your way.

JULIAN: You're kind.

MISS ALICE: But, tell me: why did you not become a priest? Having gone so far, I should think . . .

JULIAN: A lay brother serves.

MISS ALICE: . . . but is not ordained, is more a servant.

JULIAN: The house of God is so grand . . . [*sweet apologetic smile*] it needs many servants.

MISS ALICE: How humble. But is that the only reason?

JULIAN: I am not wholly reconciled. Man's God and mine are not . . . close friends.

MISS ALICE: Indeed. But, tell me, how are you not certain that you have slept with a woman?

JULIAN [*with curiosity*]: Shall I tell you? We have many more important matters. . . .

MISS ALICE: Tell me, please. The money will not run off. Great wealth is patient.

JULIAN: I would not know. Very well. It's good for me, I think, to talk about it. The institution . . . to which I committed myself – it was deep inland, by the way – was a good one, good enough, and had, as I am told most do, sections – buildings, or floors of buildings – for patients in various conditions . . . some for violent cases, for example, others for children. . . .

MISS ALICE: How sad.

JULIAN: Yes. Well, at any rate . . . sections. Mine . . . my section was for people who were . . . mildly troubled – which I found ironic, for I have never considered the fleeing of faith a mild matter. Nonetheless, for the mildly troubled. The windows were not barred; one was allowed utensils, and one's own clothes. You see, escape was not a matter of urgency, for it was a section for mildly troubled people who had committed themselves, and should escape occur, it was not a danger for the world outside.

MISS ALICE: I understand.

JULIAN: There was a period during my stay, however, when I began to . . . hallucinate, and to withdraw, to a point where I was not entirely certain when my mind was tricking me, or when it was not. I believe one would say – how is it said? – that my grasp on reality was . . . tenuous – occasionally. There was, at the same time, in my section, a woman who, on very infrequent occasions, believed that she was the Virgin Mary.

MISS ALICE [*mild surprise*]: My goodness.

JULIAN: A quiet woman, plain, but soft features, not hard; at forty, or a year either side, married, her husband the owner of a dry-goods store, if my memory is correct; childless . . . the sort of woman, in short, that one is not aware of passing on the street, or in a hallway . . . unlike you – if you will permit me.

MISS ALICE [*smiles*]: It may be I am . . . noticeable, but almost never identified.

JULIAN: You shun publicity.

MISS ALICE: Oh, indeed. And I have few friends . . . that, too, by choice. [*Urges him on with a gesture.*] But please . . .

JULIAN: Of course. My hallucinations . . . were saddening to me. I suspect I should have been frightened of them – as well as by them – most people are, or would be . . . by hallucinations. But I was . . . saddened. They were, after all, provoked, brought on by the departure of my faith, and this in turn was brought on by the manner in which people mock God. . . .

MISS ALICE: I notice you do not say you lost your faith, but that it abandoned you.

JULIAN: Do I. Perhaps at bottom I had lost it, but I think more that I was confused . . . *and* intimidated . . . by the world about me, and let slip contact with it . . . with my faith. So, I was *sad*dened.

MISS ALICE: Yes.

JULIAN: The periods of hallucination would be announced by a ringing in the ears, which produced, or was accompanied by, a loss of hearing. I would hear people's voices from a great distance and through the roaring of . . . surf. And my body would feel light, and not mine, and I would float – no, glide.

MISS ALICE: There was no feeling of terror in this? I would be beside myself.

JULIAN: No, as I said, sadness. Aaaaahhh, I would think, I am going from myself again. How very, very sad . . . everything. Loss, great loss.

MISS ALICE: I understand.

JULIAN: And when I was away from myself – never far enough, you know, to . . . blank, just to . . . fog over – when I was away from myself I could not sort out my imaginings from what was real. Oh, sometimes I would say to a nurse or one of the attendants, 'Could you tell me, did I preach last night? To the patients? A fire-and-brimstone lesson. Did I do that, or did I imagine it?' And they would tell me, if they knew.

MISS ALICE: And did you?

JULIAN: Hm? . . . No, it would seem I did not . . . to their knowledge. But I was never sure, you see.

MISS ALICE [*nodding*]: No.

JULIAN [*a brief, rueful laugh*]: I imagined so many things, or . . . did so many things I thought I had imagined. The uncertainty . . . you know?

MISS ALICE [*smiles*]: Are you sure you're not describing what passes for sanity?

JULIAN [*laughs briefly, ruefully*]: Perhaps. But one night . . . now, there! You see? I said 'one night,' and I'm not sure, even now, whether or not this thing happened or, if it did not happen, it did or did not happen at noon, or in the morning, much less at night . . . yet I say night. Doubtless one will do as well as another. So. One *night* the following either happened or did not happen. I was walking in the gardens – or I imagined I was walking in the gardens – walking in the gardens, and I heard a sound . . . sounds from near where a small pool stood, with rosebushes, rather overgrown, a formal garden once, the . . . the place had been an estate, I remember being told. Sounds . . . sobbing? Low cries. And there was, as well, the ringing in my ears, and . . . and fog, a . . . a milkiness, between myself and . . . everything. I went toward the cries, the sounds, and . . . I, I fear my description will become rather . . . vivid now . . . .

MISS ALICE: I am a grown woman.

JULIAN [*nods*]: Yes. [*A deep breath.*] The . . . the woman, the woman I told you about, who hallucinated, herself, that she was the Virgin . . .

MISS ALICE: Yes, yes.

JULIAN: . . . was . . . was on a grassy space by the pool – or this is what I imagined – on the ground, and she was in her . . . a nightdress, a . . . gossamer, filmy thing, or perhaps she was not, but there she was, on the ground, on an incline, a slight incline, and when she saw me – or

sensed me there – she raised her head, and put her arms
... [*Demonstrates.*] ... out, in a ... supplication, and
cried, 'Help me, help me ... help me, oh God, God,
help me ... oh, help, help.' This, over and over, and
with the sounds in her throat between. I ... I came closer,
and the sounds, her sounds, her words, the roaring in my
ears, the gossamer and the milk film, I ... a ROAR, AN
OCEAN! Saliva, perfume, sweat, the taste of blood and
rich earth in the mouth, sweet sweaty slipping ... [*looks
to her apologetically, nods*] ... ejaculation. [*She nods.*] The
sound cascading away, the rhythms breaking, everything
slowly, limpid, quieter, damper, soft ... soft, quiet ...
done. [*They are both silent.* MISS ALICE *is gripping the arms
of her chair;* JULIAN *continues softly.*] I have described it to
you, as best I can, as it ... happened, or did not happen.

MISS ALICE [*curiously ... dispassionately*]: I ... am a very
beautiful woman.

JULIAN [*after a pause which serves as reply to her statement*]: I
must tell you more, though. You *have* asked me for an
entirety.

MISS ALICE: And a very rich one.

JULIAN [*brief pause, nods*]: As I mentioned to you, the
woman was given to hallucinations as well, but perhaps
I should have said that being the Virgin Mary was merely
the strongest of her ... delusions; she ... hallucinated
... as well as the next person, about perfectly mundane
matters, too. So it may be that now we come to coinci-
dence, or it may not. Shortly – several days – after the
encounter I have described to you – the encounter which
did or did not happen – the woman ... I do not know
which word to use here, either descended or ascended into
an ecstasy, the substance of which was that she was with
child ... that she was pregnant with the Son of God.

MISS ALICE: And I live here, in all these rooms.

JULIAN: You don't laugh? Well, perhaps you will, at *me*.

I was ... beside myself, for I assumed the piling of delusion upon delusion, though the chance of there being fact, happening, there somewhere ... I went to my ... doctor and told him of my hallucination – if indeed that is what it was. He told me, then ... that the woman had been examined, that she was suffering from cancer of the womb, that it was advanced, had spread. In a month, she died.

MISS ALICE: Did you believe it?

JULIAN [*small smile*]: That she died?

MISS ALICE: That you spoke with your doctor.

JULIAN [*pause*]: It has never occurred to me until this moment to doubt it. He has informed me many times.

MISS ALICE: Ah?

JULIAN: I *do see* him ... in reality. We have become friends, we talk from time to time. Socially.

MISS ALICE: Ah. And was it he who discharged you from ... your asylum?

JULIAN: I was persuaded, eventually, that perhaps I was ... overconcerned by hallucination; that some was inevitable, and a portion of that – even desirable.

MISS ALICE: Of course.

JULIAN [*looking at his hands*]: Have I answered your question? That I am not ... sure that I have slept with a woman.

MISS ALICE [*puzzling ... slowly*]: I don't ... know. Is the memory of something having happened the same as it having happened?

JULIAN: It is not the nicest of ... occurrences – to have described to you.

MISS ALICE [*kindly*]: It was many years ago. [*Then, an afterthought.*] Was it not?

JULIAN: Yes, yes, quite a while ago.

MISS ALICE [*vaguely amused*]: I am rich and I am beautiful and I live here in all these rooms ... without relatives, with a . . . [*wry*] companion, from time to time . . . [*leans forward, whispers, but still amused*] . . . and with a secret.

JULIAN: Oh? [*Trying to be light, too.*] And may I know it? The secret?

MISS ALICE: I don't know yet.

JULIAN [*relaxing*]: Ah-ha.

MISS ALICE [*sudden change of mood, to brisk, official, cool*]: Well then. You're here on business, not for idle conversation, I believe.

JULIAN [*confused, even a little hurt*]: Oh . . . yes, that's . . . that's right.

MISS ALICE: You have instruction to give me – not formal, I'm not about to settle in your faith. Information, facts, questions and answers.

JULIAN [*slightly sour*]: Odds and ends, I believe.

MISS ALICE [*sharp*]: To you, perhaps. But important if you're to succeed, if you're not to queer the whole business, if you're not to . . .

JULIAN: Yes, yes!

MISS ALICE: So you'll be coming back here . . . when I wish to see you.

JULIAN: Yes.

MISS ALICE: Several times. It might be better if you were to move in. I'll decide it.

JULIAN: Oh . . . well, of course, if you think . . .

MISS ALICE: I think. [JULIAN *nods acquiescence.*] Very good. [SHE *rises.*] No more today, no more now.

JULIAN [*up, maybe retreating a little*]: Well, if you'll let me know when . . .

MISS ALICE: Come here. [JULIAN *goes to her; she takes his head in her hands, kisses him on the forehead, he registers embarrassment, she laughs, a slightly mocking, unnerving laugh.*] Little recluse. [*Laughs again.*]

JULIAN: If you'll . . . advise me, or His Eminence, when you'd like me to . . .

MISS ALICE: Little bird, pecking away in the library. [*Laughs again.*]

JULIAN: I'm ... disappointed you find me so ... humorous.

MISS ALICE [*cheerful, but not contrite*]: Oh, forgive me, I live so alone, the oddest things cheer me up. You ... cheer me up. [*Holds out her hand to be kissed.*] Here. [JULIAN *hesitates.*] Ah-ah-ah, he who hesitates loses all. [JULIAN *hesitates again, momentarily, then kisses her hand, but kneeling, as he would kiss a Cardinal's ring.* MISS ALICE *laughs at this.*] Do you think I am a Cardinal? Do I look like a Prince? Have you never even kissed a woman's hand?

JULIAN [*back on his feet, evenly*]: No. I have not.

MISS ALICE [*kindlier now*]: I'll send for you, we'll have ... pleasant afternoons, you and I. Goodbye.

> [MISS ALICE *turns away from* JULIAN, *gazes out a window, her back to the audience.* JULIAN *exits. The* LAWYER *enters the set from the bedroom door.*]

LAWYER [*to* MISS ALICE, *a bit abruptly*]: How did it go, eh?

MISS ALICE [*turns around, matter-of-factly*]: Not badly.

LAWYER: You took long enough.

> [MISS ALICE *shrugs.*]

When are you having him again?

MISS ALICE [*very wickedly*]: On business, or privately?

LAWYER: Don't be childish.

MISS ALICE: Whenever you like, whenever you say. [*Seriously.*] Tell me honestly, do you really think we're wise?

LAWYER: Wise? Well, we'll see. If we prove not, I can't think of anything standing in the way that can't be destroyed. [*Pause.*] Can you?

MISS ALICE [*rather sadly*]: No. Nothing.

CURTAIN

ACT TWO

Scene One

The library – as of Act One, Scene Two. No one on stage. Evening.
[MISS ALICE hurtles through the archway, half running,
half backing, with the LAWYER after her. It is not a chase;
she has just broken from him, and her hurtling is the result of
sudden freeing.]

MISS ALICE [*just before and as she is entering; her tone is neither*
hysterical nor frightened; she is furious and has been mildly
hurt]: KEEP . . . GO! GET YOUR . . . LET GO OF ME! [*She*
is in the room.] KEEP OFF! KEEP OFF ME!

LAWYER [*excited, ruffled, but trying to maintain decorum*]: Don't
be hysterical, now.

MISS ALICE [*still moving away from him, as he comes on*]: KEEP
. . . AWAY. JUST STAY AWAY FROM ME.

LAWYER: I said don't be hysterical.

MISS ALICE: I'll *show* you hysteria. I'll give you *fireworks!*
KEEP! Keep away.

LAWYER [*soothing, but always moving in on her*]: A simple
touch, an affectionate hand on you; nothing more . . .

MISS ALICE [*quiet loathing*]: You're degenerate.

LAWYER [*steely*]: An affectionate hand, in the privacy of a
hallway . . .

MISS ALICE [*almost a shriek*]: THERE ARE PEOPLE!!

LAWYER: Where? There are no people.

MISS ALICE [*between her teeth*]: There are people.

LAWYER [*feigning surprise*]: There are no people. [*To a*
child.] Ahh! [*Walks toward the model, indicates it.*] Unless
you mean all the little people running around inside here.
Is that what you mean?

MISS ALICE [*a mirthless, don't-you-know-it laugh*]: Hunh-hunh-
hunh-hunh.

LAWYER: Is that who you mean? All the little people in
here? [*Change of tone to normal, if sarcastic.*] Why don't we
show them a few of your tricks, hunh?

MISS ALICE [*moving away, clenched teeth again*]: Keep . . .
away . . . . from . . . me.

LAWYER [*without affection*]: To love is to possess, and since
I desire to possess you, that must mean conversely that I
love you, must it not. Come here.

MISS ALICE [*with great force*]: PEOPLE!

LAWYER: Your little priest? Your little Julian? He is
not . . .

MISS ALICE: He is not a priest!

LAWYER: No. And he is not near by – momentarily!
[*Hissed.*] I am sick of him here day after day, sick of the
time you're taking. Will you get it done with!

MISS ALICE: No! He will be *up*.

LAWYER: Oh, for Christ's sake, he's a connoisseur; he'll
be nosing around the goddam wine cellar for hours!

MISS ALICE: He will be *up*. [*Afterthought.*] Butler!

LAWYER [*advancing*]: Butler? Let him watch. [*A sneer.*]
Which is something I've been meaning to discuss with
you for the longest time now. . . .

MISS ALICE [*calm, quivering hatred; almost laughing with it*]: I
have a loathing for you that I can't de*scribe*.

LAWYER: You were never one with words. [*Suddenly
brutal.*] NOW, COME HERE.

MISS ALICE [*shrugs*]: All right. I won't react, I promise
you.

LAWYER [*beginning to fondle her*]: Won't react . . . indeed.
[*During this next, MISS ALICE is backed up against something, and the LAWYER is calmly at her, kissing her neck,
fondling her. She is calm, and at first he seems amused.*]

MISS ALICE: What causes this loathing I have for you?

It's the *way* you have, I suppose; the clinical way; methodical, slow . . .

LAWYER: . . . thorough . . .

MISS ALICE: . . . uninvolved . . .

LAWYER: . . . oh, very involved . . .

MISS ALICE: . . . impersonality in the most personal things . . .

LAWYER: . . . your passivity is exciting . . .

MISS ALICE: . . . passive only to some people . . . [*he nips her*] OW.

LAWYER: A little passion; good.

MISS ALICE [*as he continues fondling her; perhaps by the end he has her dress off her shoulders*]: With so much . . . many things to loathe, I must choose carefully, to impress you most with it.

LAWYER: Um-humh.

MISS ALICE: Is it the hair? Is it the hair on your back I loathe most? Where the fat lies, on your shoulderblades, the hair on your back . . . black, ugly? . . .

LAWYER: But too short to get a hold on, eh?

MISS ALICE: Is it that – the back hair? It could be; it would be enough. Is it your . . . . what is the polite word for it . . . your sex?

LAWYER [*mocking*]: Careful now, with a man's pride.

MISS ALICE: Ugly: that too – ugly.

LAWYER [*unruffled*]: Better than most, if you care for a *man* . . .

MISS ALICE: . . . ugly coarse uncut ragged . . . PUSH!

LAWYER: Push . . . yes . . .

MISS ALICE: . . . selfish, hurtful, ALWAYS! OVER AND OVER!

LAWYER: You like it; it feels good.

MISS ALICE [*very calm and analytical*]: But is that what I loathe most? It could be; that would be enough, too.

LAWYER: . . . oh, what a list . . .

MISS ALICE: But I think it is most the feel of your skin . . .
[*Hard.*] that you can't sweat.
  [*He stiffens some.*]
That your body is as impersonal as your . . . self – dry,
uncaring, rubbery . . . dead. Ah . . . there . . . that is
what I loathe about you most: you're dead. Moving
pushing selfish dry dead. [*Brief pause.*] Does that hurt?
Does something finally, beautifully hurt? [*Self-mocking
laugh.*] Have I finally gotten . . . into you?

LAWYER [*a little away from her now*]: Insensitive, still, aren't
you, after all this time. Does it hurt? Does something
finally hurt?

MISS ALICE: . . . deep, gouging hurt?

LAWYER: Everything! Everything in the day and night,
eating, resting, walking, rutting, everything! Everything
hurts.

MISS ALICE: Awwwwww.

LAWYER: Inside the . . . sensibility, everything hurts.
Deeply.

MISS ALICE [*ridiculing*]: And is that why I loathe you?

LAWYER [*a quiet, rueful laugh*]: Probably. [*Quickly back to
himself.*] But you, little playmate, you're what I want
now. GIVE!

MISS ALICE: If Julian comes in here . . .

LAWYER [*shoves her*]: Are you playing it straight, hunh?
Or do you like your work a little bit, hunh? [*Again.*] Do
you enjoy spreading your legs for the clergy? [*Again.*]
Hunh?

MISS ALICE: STOP! . . . YOU!

LAWYER: Is that our private donation to the Church?
Our own grant? YES? [*Begins to hurt her arm.*] Are we plan-
ning to turn into a charitable, educational foundation?

MISS ALICE [*in pain*]: My arm!
  [BUTLER *enters, unnoticed; watches.*]

LAWYER [*hard and very serious*]: Don't you dare mess this

thing up. You behave the way I've told you; you PLAY-
ACT. You do your part; STRAIGHT.

BUTLER [*calmly*]: Brother Julian . . .

MISS ALICE: Butler! Help me!

BUTLER [*as the* LAWYER *releases her*]: . . . has now examined
the wine cellar, with awe and much murmuring, and
will be with us presently. He's peeing. So I suggest –
unless you're doing this for his benefit – uh, you stop.

MISS ALICE [*as she and the* LAWYER *pull themselves together*]:
He hurt me, Butler.

BUTLER [*calmly, as if reminding her*]: Often. [*To the* LAWYER,
with mock friendliness.] Up to your old tricks, eh?

LAWYER [*dusting himself off*]: She is . . . not behaving.

BUTLER [*very noncommittal*]: Ah me.

MISS ALICE [*under her breath, to the* LAWYER]: Savage!
[*Realizes.*] Both of you!

LAWYER [*laughs*]: The maiden in the shark pond.

MISS ALICE: He thinks I'm sleeping with Julian. [*To*
LAWYER.] You poor jealous . . .

BUTLER: Are you?

MISS ALICE [*indignant*]: No! [*Almost sad about it.*] No, I
am not.

LAWYER: She is!

MISS ALICE: I said I am not!

BUTLER: Are you going to?

MISS ALICE [*after a pause; to* LAWYER]: Am I going to?
Am I going to . . . spread my legs for the clergy? Enjoy
my work a little? Isn't that what you'd have me do? To
not mess it up? To play my part straight? Isn't that what
you'll HAVE ME DO?

LAWYER: You don't need urging! . . .

BUTLER: Now, children . . .

MISS ALICE: When the time comes? Won't you have me
at him? Like it or not? Well . . . I will like it!

[*A little hard breathing from* MISS ALICE *and the* LAWYER.]

BUTLER: Something *should* be done about the wine cellar. I've noticed it – as a passerby would – but Brother Julian pointed out the extent of it to me: bottles have burst, are bursting, corks rotting . . . something to do with the temperature or the dampness. It's a shame, you know.

MISS ALICE [*surprisingly shrill*]: Well, fix it!

BUTLER [*ignoring her tone*]: Some great years, popping, dribbling away, going to vinegar under our feet. There is a Mouton Rothschild – one I'm especially fond of – that's . . .

LAWYER [*pacifying*]: Do. Do . . . fix it.

BUTLER [*shakes his head*]: Going. All of it. Great shame.

LAWYER: Yes, yes.

BUTLER [*brightly*]: Nice thing about having Julian here so much . . . he's helpful. Wines, plants . . . do you know, he told me some astonishing things about ferns. We were in the solarium . . .

MISS ALICE [*quiet pleading*]: Please . . . stop.

BUTLER: Oh. Well, it's nice having him about.

LAWYER [*sour*]: Oh, we'll be a foursome very soon.

MISS ALICE [*brightly*]: Yes.

LAWYER [*with a mirthless smile*]: Warning.

BUTLER [*cheerful again*]: It *would* be a great deal more sensible than . . . puttering out here every day. We could put him over the chapel! Now, that's a splendid idea. He likes the chapel, he said, not resonant, too small or something, wrong angles, but he likes it . . .

MISS ALICE: When he moves here . . .

LAWYER: He will move here when I say – and as I say.

MISS ALICE [*fake smile*]: We shall see.

LAWYER [*still offhand*]: We shall not see.

JULIAN [*offstage*]: Halloo!

BUTLER: In . . . in here.

MISS ALICE [sotto voce *to the* LAWYER]: You say we shall not see? *Shall* we?

LAWYER [*as above*]: Warning.
> [JULIAN enters.]

JULIAN: Ah! There you all are.

LAWYER: *We* had wondered where *you* were.

MISS ALICE [*reminding a child*]: You usually find us here after dinner.

JULIAN: Yes, and a superb dinner.

LAWYER: . . . and then Butler reminded us that you were in the cellar.

JULIAN [*sincere, but prepared*]: Miss Alice, your . . . home possesses two things that, were I a designer of houses – for the very wealthy, of course – I would put in all my designs.

MISS ALICE [*smiling*]: And what are they?

LAWYER [*to* MISS ALICE, *mildly mocking* JULIAN]: Can't you guess?

MISS ALICE [*charmingly*]: Of course I can guess, but I want Julian to have the pleasure of saying it.

JULIAN: A chapel and a wine cellar.

MISS ALICE [*agreeing, but is she making light fun?*]: Yes.

LAWYER: We hear, though, that the wine cellar is a wreck. And aren't there cobwebs in the chapel, too?

JULIAN [*light but standing up to him*]: One or two spiders have been busy around the altar, and the organ is . . . in need of use . . .

LAWYER [*very funny to him*]: HUNH!

JULIAN [*choosing to ignore it*]: . . . but it *is* a chapel, a good one. The wine cellar, however . . . [*shakes his head*] . . . great, great shame.

BUTLER: Exactly my words.

MISS ALICE: Well, we must have it tended to – and especially since you are our guest so frequently these days, and enjoy good wines.

JULIAN: I would call someone in, a specialist, if I were you.

LAWYER [*patronizing*]: Why? Can't you take care of it? Your domain?

JULIAN [*quietly*]: The chapel, more, I should think.

BUTLER: Where does the Church get its wine . . . for Communion and the like?

JULIAN: Oh, it is grown, *made* . . . grown, the grapes, harvested, pressed . . . by, by monks.

LAWYER [*false heartiness*]: A regular profit-making setup, the Church.

JULIAN [*quietly, as usual*]: Self-sustaining . . . in some areas.

LAWYER: But not in others, eh? Sometimes the old beggar bell comes out, doesn't it? Priest as leper.

MISS ALICE [*mildly to* LAWYER]: It *is* true: you are not fit for God's sight.

BUTLER [*to the* LAWYER; *cheerfully interested*]: Is that *so*! I wasn't sure.

LAWYER [*to* MISS ALICE, *feigning curiosity and surprise*]: Who whispered it to you?

MISS ALICE [*indicating* JULIAN. *Semi-serious*]: My confessor.

LAWYER [*a sneer; to* Julian]: Did you? And so *you* object, as well? To my mention of the Church as solicitor.

JULIAN: In England I believe *you* would be referred to as solicitor.

LAWYER: No, I would not. And we are not in England . . . are we?

BUTLER: This *place* was . . . in England.

MISS ALICE [*as if suddenly remembering*]: Yes, it was! Every stone, marked and shipped.

JULIAN: Oh; I had thought it was a replica.

LAWYER: Oh no; that would have been too simple. Though it *is* a replica . . . in its way.

JULIAN: Of?

LAWYER [*pointing to the model*]: Of that. [JULIAN *laughs a little; the* LAWYER *shrugs.*] Ah well.

JULIAN [*to* MISS ALICE]: Did your . . . did your father have it . . . put up? [*A parenthesis.*] It suddenly occurred to me that I know nothing of your family, though I . . . I don't mean to pry. . . .

MISS ALICE [*a private laugh*]: No, we must not . . . well, should we say that? That my father put it up? No. Let us not say that.

BUTLER [*to* JULIAN, *pointing first to the model, then to the room*]: Do you mean the model . . . or the replica?

JULIAN: I mean the . . . I mean . . . what we are in.

BUTLER: *Ah*-ha. And which is that?

JULIAN: That we are in?

BUTLER: Yes.

LAWYER [*to* JULIAN]: You are clearly not a Jesuit. [*Turning.*] Butler, you've put him in a clumsy trap.

BUTLER [*shrugging*]: I'm only a servant.

LAWYER [*to* JULIAN, *too sweetly*]: You needn't accept his alternative . . . that since we are clearly not in a model we must be in a replica.

BUTLER [*vaguely annoyed*]: Why must he not accept that?

MISS ALICE: Yes. Why not?

LAWYER: I said he did not *need* to accept the alternative. I did not say it was not valid.

JULIAN [*cheerfully*]: I will not accept it; the problem is only semantic.

BUTLER [*perhaps too consoling*]: Well, yes; that's what I would have thought.

LAWYER: Not necessarily, though. Depends, doesn't it, on your concept of reality, on the limit of possibilities. . . .

MISS ALICE [*genuinely put off*]: Oh, Lord!

LAWYER: There are no limits to possibi . . . [*Suddenly embarrassed.*] I'm . . . I'm sorry.

MISS ALICE [*to* JULIAN, *but at the* LAWYER]: He starts in, he *will*; give him the most sophomoric conundrum, and he'll bore you to death.

LAWYER [*violently*]: I! Will! Not!

JULIAN [*to break the silence*]: Well . . . perhaps I'm at fault here.

MISS ALICE [*quietly, kindly*]: How could you be? . . . Dear Julian.

LAWYER [*to* MISS ALICE; *burning*]: I thought I had educated you; I thought I had drilled you sufficiently in matters of consequence; [*Growing louder.*] I thought I had made it clear to you the way you were to behave.

JULIAN: Perhaps I should leave now; I think that . . .

LAWYER: DON'T INTERRUPT ME! [*Glares at* JULIAN, *who moves off to the model.*]

MISS ALICE [*to the* LAWYER; *calmly*]: You forget your place.

LAWYER [*clearly trying to get hold of himself*]: I . . . you . . . are quite right . . . Miss Alice, and abstractions *are* upsetting.

MISS ALICE [*to the* LAWYER; *patiently*]: Perhaps you'll go home now.

BUTLER [*cheerfully*]: Shall I have your car brought around?

LAWYER [*trying to be private in public*]: I . . . I thought that with so much to attend to, I might . . . spend the night. Of course, if you'd rather I didn't . . . [*Leaves it unfinished.* MISS ALICE *smiles enigmatically.*]

BUTLER [*pretending to think the remark was for him*]: I don't *mind* whether you do or not.

JULIAN [*peering at the model, rather amazed*]: Can it . . . can it be?

LAWYER: In the heat of . . . I, I forgot myself.

MISS ALICE [*patronizingly sweet*]: Yes.

LAWYER [*matter-of-fact*]: You will forgive me.

MISS ALICE [*toying*]: Oh?

BUTLER: Shall I have his car brought around?

LAWYER [*sudden softening*]: Let me stay.

JULIAN [*shy attempt at getting attention*]: Please . . .

MISS ALICE [*malicious pleasure in it*]: I don't know . . .

JULIAN [*more urgently*]: Please!

LAWYER [*bitter*]: As you wish, of course. [*Swings his hand back as if to strike her; she flinches.*]

JULIAN: PLEASE!

BUTLER [*patiently amused curiosity*]: What *is* it, for heaven's sake?

JULIAN [*pointing to the model*]: The model is . . . on fire; it's on fire!

BUTLER [*urgent dropping of butlerish attitudes*]: Where!

LAWYER: Good Christ!

MISS ALICE: Quick!

[*The* LAWYER *and* BUTLER *rush to the model.*]

BUTLER: *Where*, for Christ's sake!

JULIAN [*jostled*]: In the . . . over the . . .

LAWYER: Find it!

BUTLER [*peering into various windows with great agitation*]: It's . . . it's the . . . where the hell is it! . . . It's the . . . chapel! The chapel's burning!

MISS ALICE: Hurry!

BUTLER: Come on! Let's get to it! [*Begins to run out of the room.*] Are you coming? Julian!

JULIAN [*confused, but following*]: But I . . , but . . . yes, of course.

[JULIAN *and* BUTLER *run out.*]

MISS ALICE [*to the* LAWYER *as he hangs back*]: We're burning down! Hurry!

LAWYER [*comes up to her, grabs her by the wrist, forces her to the ground, keeps hold*]: Burning down? Consumed? WHY NOT! Remember what I told you. Watch . . . your . . . step!

[*He runs out after the others.* MISS ALICE *is left alone; maybe we hear one or two diminishing shouts from the others, offstage. Finally, silence.* MISS ALICE *doesn't rise from the floor, but gradually assumes a more natural position on it.*]

MISS ALICE [*she alternates between a kind of incantation-prayer*

and a natural tone]: [*Prayer.*] Let the fire be put out. Let
the chapel be saved; let the fire not spread; let us not be
consumed. [*Natural.*] He hurt me. My wrist hurts. Who
was the boy when I was little hurt my wrist? I don't
remember. [*Prayer.*] Let the fire not spread; let them be
quick. [*Natural.*] YOU PIG! [*Softly, almost a whine.*] You
hurt my wrist. [*Imitates the* LAWYER's *tone.*] Watch . . .
. . . your . . . step. [*Prayer.*] Oh God, I have watched my
step. I have . . . trod . . . so carefully. [*Natural and weary.*]
Let it all come down – let the whole place . . . go. [*She
must now, when using a natural tone, almost give the suggestion
of talking to someone in the model. Natural.*] I don't mean
that. I don't remember his name . . . or his face; merely
the hurt . . . and that continues, the hurt the same, the
name and the face changing, but it doesn't matter. Let
them save it. [*Prayer.*] Let them save it. Don't . . . destroy.
Let them save the resonance. [*Natural.*] Increase it.
Julian says there is no resonance, that it's not right.
[*Prayer.*] Let the resonance increase. [*Natural; a little-girl
tone.*] I have tried very hard to be careful, to obey, to
withhold my . . . nature? I have tried so hard to be good,
but I'm . . . such a stranger . . . here. [*Prayer.*] I have
tried to obey what I have not understood, understanding
that I must obey. Don't destroy! I have tried! TRIED.
[*Natural.*] Is that the way about hurt? That *it* does not
change . . . but merely its agents?

   [JULIAN *appears, unseen by* MISS ALICE.]
[*Natural, still.*] I will hold on. [*Sweetly, apologetically.*] I
will try to hold on. [*Prayer.*] I will try to hold on! [*Natural.*]
Please, please . . . if you *do* . . . be generous and gentle
with me, or . . . just gentle.

JULIAN [*softly, a little sadly*]: I don't understand anything.
The chapel was in flames.

MISS ALICE: Yes.

JULIAN: . . . and yet . . . I saw the fire here in the model . . .

and yet . . . the real chapel was in flames. We put it out.
And now the fire here is out as well.

MISS ALICE [*preceded by a brief, hysterical laugh*]: . . . yes.

JULIAN [*underneath the wonder, some fear*]: I don't understand.

MISS ALICE [*she is shivering a little*]: It's very hard. Is the
chapel saved?

JULIAN [*his attention on the model*]: Hm? Oh, yes . . . partially,
mostly. The . . . the boards, floorboards, around the altar
were . . . gave way, were burned through. The altar . . .
sank, some, angled down into the burned-through floor.
Marble.

MISS ALICE [*almost a whisper*]: But the fire is out.

JULIAN: Yes. Out. The spiders, burned to a crisp, I should
say, curled-up, burned balls. [*Asking the same question.*]
I . . . I don't understand.

MISS ALICE [*vaguely to the model*]: It is all well. We are
not . . . consumed.

JULIAN: Miss Alice? Why, why did it happen that way –
in both dimensions?

MISS ALICE [*her arms out to him*]: Help me.

    [JULIAN *goes to her, lifts her by the arms; they stand, at
arm's length, holding hands, facing each other.*]

JULIAN: Will you . . . tell me anything?

MISS ALICE [*a helpless laugh, though sad*]: I don't know anything.

JULIAN: But you were . . . [*Stops.*]

MISS ALICE [*pleading*]: I don't *know* anything.

JULIAN [*gently, to placate*]: Very well.

MISS ALICE [*coming closer to him*]: Come stay.

JULIAN: Miss Alice?

MISS ALICE: Come stay here. It will . . . be easier. For you.

JULIAN [*concern, not anger*]: Did he hurt you?

MISS ALICE: Easier than going back and forth. And for me,
too.

JULIAN: Did he?

MISS ALICE [*after a pause and a sad smile*]: Some. You're shivering, Julian.

JULIAN: No, Miss Alice, it is *you* . . . you are shivering.

MISS ALICE: The Cardinal will agree to it.

JULIAN [*looking toward the model*]: Yes, I . . . suppose so.

MISS ALICE: Are you frightened, Julian?

JULIAN: Why, no, I . . . I *am* shivering, am I not?

MISS ALICE: Yes.

JULIAN: But I am not . . . yes, I suppose I am . . . frightened.

MISS ALICE: Of what, Julian?

JULIAN [*looks toward the model again*]: But there is . . . [*back*] . . . of what.

MISS ALICE: Yes.

JULIAN [*knowing there is*]: Is there anything to be frightened of, Miss Alice?

MISS ALICE [*after a long pause*]: Always.

CURTAIN

Scene Two

The library – as of Act One, Scene Two.
    [*The* BUTLER *is on stage. The* LAWYER *enters immediately, angry, impatient.*]

LAWYER: Well, where are they today?
BUTLER [*calm, uninvolved*]: Hm? Who?
LAWYER: WHERE IS SHE! Where is she off to now?
BUTLER: Miss Alice? Well, I don't really know. [*Thinks about it.*] You look around?
LAWYER: They're not here.
BUTLER: You don't think they've eloped, do you?
LAWYER: Do you know!
BUTLER: They're moving together nicely; the fire in the chapel helped, I thought, though maybe it was intended to . . . brought them closer.
LAWYER: Where are they!
BUTLER: They spend so much time together now; everything on schedule.
LAWYER: Where have they gone!
BUTLER: I don't *know*; really. Out walking? In the gardens? Driving somewhere? Picnicking, maybe? Cold chicken, cheese, a Montrachet under an elm? I don't *know* where they are.
LAWYER: Don't you watch them?
BUTLER: Keep one eye peeled? Can't she take care of herself? She knows her business. [*Pause; then, quietly meaningful.*] Doesn't she. [*No answer.*] Doesn't she.
LAWYER: You should watch them. We don't want . . . error. She is . . .

BUTLER: Human? Yes, and clever, too . . . isn't she. *Good* at it, wrapping around fingers, enticing, I recall.

LAWYER: *Too* human; not playing it straight.

BUTLER: Enjoying her work a little? They're not sleeping together yet.

LAWYER: NO! NOT YET!

BUTLER [*a quiet warning*]: Well, it won't bother you when they do . . . will it.

LAWYER [*matter-of-factly*]: I, too: human.

BUTLER: Human, but dedicated.

LAWYER [*quiet, sick loathing*]: He doesn't deserve her.

BUTLER [*kindly*]: Well, he'll not have her long.

LAWYER [*weary*]: No; not long.

BUTLER: On . . . and on . . . we go.

LAWYER [*sad*]: Yes.

BUTLER [*too offhand, maybe*]: I've noticed, you've let your feelings loose lately; too much: possessiveness, jealousy.

LAWYER: I'm *sorry*.

BUTLER: You used to be so good.

LAWYER: I'm SORRY!

BUTLER: It's all right; just watch it.

LAWYER: Attrition: the toll time takes.

BUTLER: I watch you carefully – you, too – and it's the oddest thing: you're a cruel person, straight through; it's not cover; you're hard and cold, saved by dedication; just that.

LAWYER [*soft sarcasm*]: Thank you.

BUTLER: You're welcome, but what's happened is you're acting like the man you wish you were.

LAWYER: Yes?

BUTLER: Feeling things you can't feel. Why don't you mourn for what you are? There's lament enough there.

LAWYER [*a sad discovery*]: I've never liked you.

BUTLER [*a little sad, too*]: I don't mind. We get along. The three of us.

LAWYER: She's *using* Julian! To humiliate me.

BUTLER [*nodding*]: Of course. Humiliate; not hurt. Well, let her do her job the way she wants; she'll lead him, bring him around to it.

LAWYER: But she *cares* for him.

BUTLER: *Of* course; human, a woman. Cares, but it won't get in the way. Let her use what she can. It will be done. Don't you think it's time you went to see His Holiness again?

LAWYER: Eminence, not Holiness. You think it's time I went again? Yes; well, it *is* time. You come, too.

BUTLER [*mildly taunting*]: But shouldn't I stay here . . . to watch? To fill you in on the goings on? To let you be the last to know?

LAWYER: YOU COME! To back me up, when I want emphasis.

BUTLER: In the sense that my father used the word? Wants emphasis: lacks emphasis?

LAWYER: No. The touch of the proletarian: your simplicity, guilelessness . . .

BUTLER: Aw . . .

LAWYER: His Eminence is a pompous ass.

BUTLER: Stupid? I doubt *that*.

LAWYER: Not stupid; an ass.

BUTLER: Cardinals aren't stupid; takes brains to get there; no jokes in the Church.

LAWYER: Pompous!

BUTLER: Well, in front of you, maybe. Maybe has to wear a face; you're not easy. What will you tell him?

LAWYER: What will I tell him? Tell me.

BUTLER: All right. You play Cardinal, I'll play you.

LAWYER [*goes into it eagerly; with a laugh*]: Ah, two of you. We are doubly honoured. Will you not sit?

BUTLER: Really? Like that?

LAWYER: And how is our Brother Julian faring . . . in the world of the moneyed and the powerful?

BUTLER: No. Really?

LAWYER: Really! And can we be of service to you, further service?

BUTLER: Maybe.

LAWYER: Maybe? Ah?

BUTLER: Yes, your Brother Julian is going to be taken from you.

LAWYER: Our Brother Julian? Taken? From us?

BUTLER: Come on, Your Eminence.

LAWYER: This is a . . . preposterous . . . We . . . we don't understand you.

BUTLER: Isn't the grant enough? Isn't a hundred million a year for twenty years enough? For one man? He's not even a priest.

LAWYER [*as the* CARDINAL]: A man's soul, Sir! [*Himself.*] Not his soul, mustn't say that to him.

BUTLER [*musing*]: Shall we be dishonest? Well, then, I suppose you'll have to tell him more. Tell him the whole thing.

LAWYER [*himself*]: I will like that. It will blanch his goddam robes . . . turn 'em white.

BUTLER [*chuckles*]: Nice when you can enjoy your work, isn't it? Tell him that Julian is leaving him. That Julian has found what he's after. [*Walks to the model, indicates it.*] And I suppose you'd better tell him about . . . this, too.

LAWYER: The wonders of the world?

BUTLER: I think he'd better know . . . about this.

LAWYER: Shatter.

BUTLER: And, you know what I think would be a lovely touch?

LAWYER [*a quiet smile that is also a grimace*]: Tell me.

BUTLER: How eager you are. I think it would be a lovely touch were the Cardinal to marry them, to perform the wedding, to marry Julian to . . .

LAWYER: Alice.

BUTLER: *Miss* Alice.

LAWYER: Alice!

BUTLER: Well, all right; one through the other. But have him marry them.

LAWYER [*smiles a little*]: It would be nice.

BUTLER: I thought so.

LAWYER: But *shall* we tell him the whole thing? The Cardinal? What is happening?

BUTLER: How much can he take?

LAWYER: He is a man of God, however much he simplifies, however much he worships the symbol and not the substance.

BUTLER: Like everyone.

LAWYER: Like most.

BUTLER: Julian can't stand that; he told me so: men make God in their own image, he said. Those six years I told you about.

LAWYER: Yes. When he went into an asylum. YES.

BUTLER: It was – because he could not stand it, wasn't it? The use men put God to.

LAWYER: It's perfect; wonderful.

BUTLER: Could not reconcile.

LAWYER: No.

BUTLER: God as older brother, scout leader, couldn't take that.

LAWYER: And still not reconciled.

BUTLER: Has pardoned men, I think. Is walking on the edge of an abyss, but is balancing. Can be pushed . . . over, back to the asylums.

LAWYER: Or over . . . to the Truth. [*Addressing* JULIAN, *as if he were there; some thunder in the voice.*] God, Julian? Yes? God? *Whose* God? Have you pardoned men their blasphemy, Julian? Have you forgiven them?

BUTLER [*quiet echoing answers; being* JULIAN]: No, I

have not, have not really; have *let* them, but cannot accept.

LAWYER: Have not forgiven. No, Julian. Could you ever?

BUTLER [*ibid.*]: It is their comfort; my agony.

LAWYER: Soft God? The servant? Gingerbread God with the raisin eyes?

BUTLER [*ibid.*]: I cannot accept it.

LAWYER: Then don't accept it, Julian.

BUTLER: But there is *something*. There is a *true* God.

LAWYER: There is an abstraction, Julian, but it cannot be understood. You cannot worship it.

BUTLER [*ibid.*]: There is more.

LAWYER: There is Alice, Julian. That can be understood. Only the mouse in the model. Just that.

BUTLER [*ibid.*]: There must be more.

LAWYER: The mouse. Believe it. Don't personify the abstraction, Julian, limit it, demean it. Only the mouse, the toy. And that does not exist . . . but is all that can be worshipped. . . . Cut off from it, Julian, ease yourself, ease off. No trouble now; accept it.

BUTLER [*talking to* JULIAN *now*]: Accept it, Julian; ease off. Worship it . . .

LAWYER: Accept it.

BUTLER [*after a pause; normal again*]: Poor, poor Julian.

LAWYER [*normal, too*]: He can make it.

BUTLER: I hope he can.

LAWYER: If not? [*Shrugs.*] *Out* with him.

BUTLER [*pause*]: You cannot tell the Cardinal . . . that.

LAWYER [*weary*]: The benefits to the Church.

BUTLER: Not simply that.

LAWYER: And a man's soul. If it be saved . . . what matter how?

BUTLER: Then we'd best go to him.

LAWYER: Yes.

BUTLER: Leave Julian to Miss Alice; he is in good hands.

LAWYER [*quiet, sick rage rising*]: But his hands . . . on her.

BUTLER [*soothing*]: Temporary . . . temporal. You'll have her back.

LAWYER [*rises*]: All right.

BUTLER: Let's go.

LAWYER [*walks to the model, addresses it; quietly, but forcefully; no sarcasm*]: Rest easy; you'll have him . . . Hum; purr; breathe; rest. You will have your Julian. Wait for him. He will be yours.

CURTAIN

Scene Three

MISS ALICE's *sitting room, as of Act One, Scene Three.*
  [JULIAN *is on stage, near the fireplace, carries a riding crop;*
  the door to the bedroom is ajar.]

JULIAN [*after a moment; over his shoulder*]: It was fun, Miss
  Alice; it was fun.

MISS ALICE [*from behind the door*]: What, Julian?

JULIAN [*turns*]: It was . . . I enjoyed it; very much.

MISS ALICE [*her head appearing from behind the door*]: Enjoyed
  what?

JULIAN: Riding; it was . . . exhilarating.

MISS ALICE: I would never have thought you rode. You
  were good. [*Disappears.*]

JULIAN [*a small, self-deprecating laugh*]: Oh. Yes. When I
  was young – a child – I knew a family who . . . kept
  horses, as a pastime, not as a business. They were moneyed
  – well, had *some*. It was one of their sons who was my
  playmate . . . and we would ride.

MISS ALICE [*still behind the door*]: Yes.

JULIAN: You remember, you know how seriously children
  talk, the cabalas we have . . . had. My friend and I would
  take two hunters, and we would go off for hours, and talk
  ourselves into quite a state – mutually mesmerizing,
  almost an hysteria. We would forget the time, and bring
  the animals back quite lathered. [*Laughs.*] We would be
  scolded – no: cursed *out* – by one groom or another;
  usually by a great dark Welshman – a young fellow who
  always scowled and had – I remember it clearly, for I
  found it remarkable – the hairiest hands I have ever

seen, with hair – and this is what I found most remarkable – tufts of coarse black hair on his thumbs. [*Looks at his own thumbs.*] Not down, or a few hairs, which many of us have, but tufts. This Welshman.

MISS ALICE [*head appearing again*]: D. H. Lawrence.

JULIAN: Pardon?

MISS ALICE [*appearing, wearing a black negligee with great sleeves*]: 'Love on the Farm'. Don't you know it? [*Circles him as she recites it; mock-stalks him.*]

'I hear his hand on the latch, and rise from my chair
Watching the door open . . .
He flings the rabbit soft on the table board
And comes toward me: he! the uplifted sword
Of his hand against my bosom! . . .
. . . With his hand he turns my face to him
And caresses me with his fingers that still smell grim
Of rabbit's fur! . . .
And down his mouth comes on my mouth! and down
His bright dark eyes over me . . .
. . . his lips meet mine, and a flood
Of sweet fire sweeps across me, so I drown
Against him, die and find death good!'
[*Cocks her head, smiles.*] No?

JULIAN [*embarrassed*]: That was . . . not quite my reaction.

MISS ALICE [*a great, crystal laugh*]: No! Silly Julian! No. [*Conspiratorial.*] That was a verse I knew at school, that I memorized. 'And down his mouth comes on my mouth.' Oh! That would excite us so . . . at school; things like that. [*Normal tone; a shrug, a smile.*] Early eroticism; mental sex play.

JULIAN [*still embarrassed*]: Yes.

MISS ALICE: I've embarrassed you!

JULIAN: No! No!

MISS ALICE: Poor Julian; I have. And you were telling me about horseback riding.

JULIAN: No, I was telling you about the groom, as far as that goes. And I suppose ... yes, I suppose ... those thumbs were ... erotic for *me* – at that time, if you think about it; mental sex play. Unconscious.

MISS ALICE [*sweetly, to divert him*]: It *was* fun riding. *Today.*

JULIAN: Yes!

MISS ALICE: I am fond of hair – man's body hair, except that on the back. [*Very offhand.*] Are you hairy, Julian?

JULIAN: I ... my chest is rather nice, but my arms are ... surprisingly hairless.

MISS ALICE: And you have no back hair.

JULIAN: Well ... do you really wish to know?

MISS ALICE [*with a laugh*]: Yes!

JULIAN [*nods in acquiescence*]: I have no ... back hair, in the usual sense – of the shoulders ...

[MISS ALICE *nods.*]

... but there is hair, at the small of the back ... rising.

MISS ALICE: Yes, yes, well, *that* is nice. [*Laughs, points to the crop.*] You're carrying the crop. Are you still in the saddle?

JULIAN [*laughing; shyly brandishing the crop*]: Are you one of Mr Lawrence's ladies? Do you like the smell of saddle soap, and shall I take my crop to you?

MISS ALICE [*briefest pause; testing*]: Would you?

JULIAN [*halfhearted laugh*]: MISS ALICE!

MISS ALICE: Nobody does things naturally any more – so few people have the grace. A man takes a whip to you – a loving whip, you understand – and you *know*, deep and sadly, that it's imitation – literary, seen. [*Intentionally too much.*] No one has the natural graces any more.

JULIAN [*putting the crop down; quietly*]: I have ... not whipped ...

MISS ALICE: But surely you have.

JULIAN [*an apology*]: I do not recall.

MISS ALICE [*expansive*]: Oh, my Julian! How many layers! Yes?

JULIAN: We . . . simplify our life . . . as we grow older.

MISS ALICE [*teasing him*]: But from understanding and acceptance; not from . . . emptying ourselves.

JULIAN: There are many ways.

MISS ALICE [*showing her outfit*]: Do you like this?

JULIAN: It is most . . . becoming.

MISS ALICE [*giggles*]: We're dressed quite alike.

JULIAN [*he, too*]: But the effect is not the same.

MISS ALICE: No. It *is* easier for you living here . . . isn't it?

JULIAN: It's . . . more than a person could want – or *should* want, which is something we must discuss.

MISS ALICE [*sensing a coming disappointment*]: Oh . . .

JULIAN: Really.

MISS ALICE [*not pleasantly*]: What do we do wrong?

JULIAN: One of the sins is gluttony . . .

MISS ALICE: Are you getting a belly?

JULIAN [*smiles, but won't be put off*]: . . . and it has many faces – or many bellies, if you wish. It's a commonplace that we can have too much of things, and I have too much . . . of comfort, of surroundings, of ease, of kindness . . . of happiness. I am filled to bursting.

MISS ALICE [*hard*]: I think perhaps you misunderstand why you're here. You're *not* here to . . . to indulge yourself, to . . .

JULIAN [*tight-lipped*]: I'm aware of that.

MISS ALICE: . . . to . . . to ease in. You're here in service to your *Church*.

JULIAN: I've not lost sight of my function.

MISS ALICE: I wonder!

JULIAN [*really quite angry*]: And *I* wonder! What's being *done* to me. Am I . . . am I being temp – tested in some fashion?

MISS ALICE [*jumping on it*]: Tempted?

JULIAN: Tested in some fashion?

MISS ALICE: TEMPTED?

JULIAN: BOTH! Tested! What! My . . . my sincerity, my
. . . my other cheek? You have allowed that . . . that *man*,
your . . . your lover, to . . . ridicule me. You have per-
*mit*ted it.

MISS ALICE: I? Permit?

JULIAN: You have allowed him to abuse me, my position,
his, the Church; you have tolerated it, and *smiled*.

MISS ALICE: Tolerate!

JULIAN: And smiled. WHY AM I BEING TESTED! . . . And
why am I being tempted? By luxury, by ease, by . . .
content . . . by things I do not care to discuss.

MISS ALICE [*unsympathetic*]: You're answerable to your own
temptations.

JULIAN: Yes?

MISS ALICE [*singsong and patronizing*]: Or God is.
[JULIAN *snorts.*]
No? God is not? Is not answerable?

JULIAN: Knows. But is not answerable. I.

MISS ALICE [*softening some*]: Then *be* answerable.

JULIAN: To my temptations, I am. [*To himself more than to
her.*] It would be so easy to . . . fall in, to . . . accept these
surroundings. Oh, life would speed by!

MISS ALICE: With all the ridicule?

JULIAN: That aside.

MISS ALICE: You *have* a friend here . . . as they put it.

JULIAN [*smiles*]: Butler. Yes; he's nice.

MISS ALICE [*a little laugh*]: I meant me.

JULIAN: Well, of *course*. . . .

MISS ALICE: Or, do you think of me otherwise? Do *I* tempt
you?

JULIAN: You, Miss Alice?

MISS ALICE: Or, is it merely the fact of temptation that
upsets you so?

JULIAN: I have longed ... to be of great service. When I was young – and very prideful – I was filled with a self-importance that was ... well disguised. Serve. That was the active word: I would serve! [*Clenches his fist.*] I would serve, and damn anyone or anything that stood in my way. I would shout my humility from the roof and break whatever rules impeded my headlong rush toward obedience. I suspect that had I joined the Trappist order, where silence is the law, I would have chattered about it endlessly. I was impatient with God's agents, and with God, too, I see it now. A ... novice porter, ripping suitcases from patrons' hands, cursing those who preferred to carry some small parcel for their own. And I was blind to my pride, and intolerant of any who did not see me as the humblest of men.

MISS ALICE [*a little malice*]: You phrase it so; I suspect you've said it before.

JULIAN: Doubtless I have. Articulate men often carry set paragraphs.

MISS ALICE: Pride still.

JULIAN: Some.

MISS ALICE: And how did your ambition sit?

JULIAN: Ambition? Was it? [MISS ALICE *displays a knee casually;* JULIAN *jumps.*] What are you doing!

MISS ALICE [*vague flirting*]: I'm ... sorry.

JULIAN: Well. Ambition, yes, I suppose – ambition to be nothing, to be least. Most obedient, humblest. How did it sit? For some, patiently, but not well. For me? Even less well. But I ... learned.

MISS ALICE: To ... subside. Is that the simplification you mentioned before? Of your life. To subside ... and vanish; to leave no memory.

JULIAN: No; I wish to leave a ... memory – of work, of things done. I've told you; I wish to be of great service, to move great events; but when it's all time for crediting,

I'd like someone to say no more than 'Ah, wasn't there someone involved in this, who brought it all about? A priest? Ah-*ha*, a *lay* brother – was that it.' [*Smiles.*] Like that. The memory of someone who helped.

MISS ALICE [*pauses, then laughs*]: You're lying!

JULIAN: I?

[*Then they both laugh, like conspiratorial children.*]

MISS ALICE: Every monster was a man first, Julian; every dictator was a colonel who vowed to retire once the revolution was done; it's so easy to postpone elections, little brother.

JULIAN: The history of the Church . . .

MISS ALICE: The history of the Church shows half its saints were martyrs, martyred either for the Church, or by it. The chronology is jammed with death-seekers and hysterics: the bloodbath to immortality, Julian. Joan was only one of the suicides.

JULIAN [*quivering with intensity*]: I WISH TO SERVE AND . . . BE FORGOTTEN.

MISS ALICE [*comes over, strokes his cheek*]: Perhaps you will, Julian.

[*He takes her hand, kisses it, puts it back on his cheek.*] Yes?

JULIAN [*guiltily*]: I wish to be of service. [*A little giggle.*] I *do*.

MISS ALICE: And be forgotten.

JULIAN: Yes.

MISS ALICE [*stroking his head*]: Not even remembered a little? By some? As a gentle man, gentle Julian . . .

JULIAN: Per . . . perhaps.

MISS ALICE: . . . my little lay brother and expert on wines; my little horseback rider and crop switcher . . .

JULIAN [*as she ruffles his hair*]: Don't . . . do that.

MISS ALICE [*ruffles harder*]: My little whipper, and RAPIST?

JULIAN [*rising, moving away*]: DON'T!

MISS ALICE [*pouting, advancing*]: Julian . . .

JULIAN: No, now; no.

MISS ALICE [*still pouting*]: Julian, come kiss me.

JULIAN: Please!

MISS ALICE [*singsong*]: Come kiss.

JULIAN [*a plea*]: Miss Alice . . . Just . . . let me do my service, and let me go.

MISS ALICE [*abruptly to business; not curt, though*]: But you're *do*ing great service. Not many people have been put in the position you've been graced by – not many. Who knows – had some lesser man than you come, some bishop, all dried and salted, clacketing phrases from memory, or . . . one of those insinuating super-salesmen your Church uses, had one of them come . . . who knows? Perhaps the whole deal would have gone out the window.

JULIAN: Surely, Miss Alice, you haven't been playing games with . . . so monumental a matter.

MISS ALICE: The rich are said to be quixotic, the very wealthy cruel, overbearing; who is to say – might not vast wealth, the insulation of it, make one quite mad? Games? Oh, no, my little Julian, there are no games played here; this is for keeps, and in dead earnest. There *are* cruelties, for the insulation breeds a strange kind of voyeurism; and there is impatience, too, over the need to accomplish what should not be explained; and, at the end of it, a madness of sorts . . . but a triumph.

JULIAN [*hands apart*]: Use me, then . . . for the triumph.

MISS ALICE [*moving on him again*]: You are *being* used, my little Julian. *I* am being used . . . my little Julian. You want to be . . . employed, do you not? Sacrificed, even?

JULIAN: I have . . . there are no secrets from you, Miss Alice . . . I have . . . dreamed of sacrifice.

MISS ALICE [*touches his neck*]: Tell me.

JULIAN: You mustn't do . . . it is not wise . . .

MISS ALICE: Tell me. [*She will circle him, touch him occasionally, kiss the back of his neck once during the next speech.*]

JULIAN: Still my pride . . . a vestige of it. [*He becomes quite by himself during this; unaware of her.*] Oh, when I was still a child, and read of the Romans, how they used the saints as playthings – enraged children gutting their teddy bears, dashing the head of their doll against the bedpost, I could . . . I could entrance myself, and see the gladiator on me, his trident fork against my neck, and hear, even hear, as much as feel, the prongs as they entered me; the . . . the beast's saliva dripping from the yellow teeth, the slack sides of the mouth, the . . . sweet, warm breath of the lion; great paws on my spread arms . . . even the rough leather of the pads; and to the point of . . . as the great mouth opened, the breath no longer warm but hot, the fangs on my jaw and forehead, positioned . . . IN. And as the fangs sank in, the great tongue on my cheek and eye, the splitting of the bone, and the *blood* . . . just before the great sound, the coming dark and the silence. I could . . . experience it all. And was . . . engulfed. [*A brief laugh, but not breaking the trance.*] Oh, martyrdom. To be that. To be able . . . to be that.

MISS ALICE [*softly, into his ear; he does not hear it*]: Marry me, Julian.

JULIAN: The . . . death of the saints . . . was always the beginning of their lives. To go bloodstained and worthy . . . upward. I could feel the blood on my robes as I went; the smell of the blood, as intense as paint . . . and warm . . . and painless.

MISS ALICE: Marry me.

JULIAN: 'Here. I have come. You see my robes? They're red, are they not? Warm? And are not the folds caught together . . . as the blood coagulates? The . . . fingers of my left hand – of both! – are . . . are hard to move apart, as the blood holds finger to finger. And there is a wound in me, the warm dark flow ... runs down my belly ... to ... bathing my groin. You see? I have come ... blood-stained and worthy.'

MISS ALICE: Marry me.

JULIAN [*still self-tranced*]: Bathed ... my groin. And as the thumbs of the gladiator pressed ... against ... my neck, I ... as the lion's belly pressed on my chest, I ... as the ... I ... or as the woman sank ... on the mossy hillock by the roses, and the roar is the crunching growl is the moan is the sweat-breathing is the ...

MISS ALICE [*behind him, her arms around his neck, on his chest*]: ... sweat-breathing on the mossy hillock and the white mist in the perfumes ...

JULIAN: ... fumes ... lying ... on the moss hill in the white filmy gladiator's belly pressing on the chest fanged and the soft hard tongue and the *blood* ... ENTERS ... [*Lurches from the chair.*] ... STOP! ... THAT!

MISS ALICE [*coming at him slowly*]: Come to Alice, Julian, in your sacrifice ...

JULIAN [*moving away, but helpless*]: Stay ... away ... stay.

MISS ALICE: ... give yourself to her, Julian ...

JULIAN: ... a ... away ...

MISS ALICE [*sweetly singsong*]: Come marry Alice, she wants you so; she says she wants you so, come give yourself to Alice; oh, Alice needs you and your sacrifice ...

JULIAN: ... no ... no ...

MISS ALICE: ... Alice says she wants you, come to Alice, Alice tells me so, she wants you, come to Alice ...

JULIAN: ... no ... sacrifice ...

MISS ALICE: Alice tells me so, instructs me, come to her. [MISS ALICE *has her back to the audience,* JULIAN *facing her, but at a distance; she takes her gown and, spreading her arms slowly, opens the gown wide; it is the unfurling of great wings.*]

JULIAN [*shaking, staring at her body*]: . . . and . . . sacrifice . . . on the altar of . . .

MISS ALICE: Come . . . come . . .

JULIAN . . . the . . . Lord . . . God . . . in . . . Heaven . . .

MISS ALICE: Come . . .

[JULIAN *utters a sort of dying cry and moves, his arms in front of him, to* MISS ALICE; *when he reaches her, she enfolds him in her great wings.*]

MISS ALICE [*soothing*]: You will be hers; you will sacrifice yourself to her . . .

JULIAN [*muffled*]: Oh my God in heaven . . .

MISS ALICE [*her head going back, calling out*]: Alice! . . . Alice? . . .

JULIAN [*slowly kneeling within the great wings*]: . . . in . . . my . . . sacrifice . . .

MISS ALICE [*still calling out*]: He will be yours! He will be yours! AAAAALLLLLIIIIICCCCCEEEEE!

CURTAIN

ACT THREE

The library, as of Act One, Scene Two. No one on stage.
>[*After a moment or so,* BUTLER *enters, carrying what looks
to be a pile of grey sheets. They are clearly quite heavy. He sets
them down on a table, straightens his shoulders from the
effort, looks at various chairs, turns to counting the pile.*
JULIAN *enters, at more than a casual pace, dressed in a suit.*]

JULIAN: Butler!
BUTLER [*deliberate pause; then*]: . . . four . . . five . . . six . . .
[*Pretending suddenly to see* JULIAN.] Oh! Hello there.
JULIAN: Where . . . I . . . I feel quite *lost*.
BUTLER [*no comment*]: Why?
JULIAN [*agitation underneath*]: Well, uh . . . I will confess I
haven't participated in . . . been married before, but . . . I
can't imagine it's usual for everyone to disap*pear*.
BUTLER: Has everyone?
JULIAN: Yes! [*Quieter.*] Yes, I . . . per – perhaps His
Eminence is occupied, or has *bus*iness – that's it! – has
business with . . . but – but why *she* should . . . There I
was . . . one moment married, flooded with white, and
. . . then . . . the next, alone. Quite alone, in the . . .
echoes.
BUTLER: There is an echo, sometimes, all through it, down
every long hall, up in the huge beams . . .
JULIAN: But to be left alone!
BUTLER: Aren't you used to that?
JULIAN: Suddenly!
BUTLER [*sad smile*]: Like a little boy? When the closet door
swings shut after him? Locking him in the dark?
JULIAN: Hm? Yes . . . yes, like that. [*Shudders a little.*]
Terrifying.

BUTLER: And it's always remote, an attic closet, where one should not have been, where no one can hear, and is not likely to come . . . for a very long time.

JULIAN [*asking him to stop*]: Yes!

BUTLER [*to the sheets again counting them*]: We learn so early . . . are *told*, where not to go, the things we should not do. And there's often a reason.

JULIAN: And *she* vanished as well.

BUTLER: Who?

JULIAN: My . . . my wife.

BUTLER: And who is that?

JULIAN [*as if* BUTLER *had forgotten everything*]: Miss Alice!

BUTLER: Ah. Really?

JULIAN: Butler, you saw the wedding!

BUTLER [*puzzles it a moment*]: Quite so; I did. We . . . Well. Perhaps Miss Alice is changing.

JULIAN: She *must* be; of course. But . . . for everyone to . . . vanish, as if I'd turned my back for a *moment*, and an hour elapsed, or a . . . dimension had . . .

BUTLER [*passing it over*]: Yes, a dimension – well, that happens.

JULIAN [*still preoccupied*]: Yes, she must be . . . upstairs. What . . . what are you doing?

BUTLER: What?

JULIAN: What are those?

BUTLER: These? [*Looks at them.*] Uh . . . sheets, or covers, more accurately.

JULIAN [*still quite nervous, staying away*]: What are they for?

BUTLER: To . . . cover.

JULIAN [*ibid.*]: Cover *what*!

BUTLER: Oh . . . nothing; no matter. Housework, that's all. One of my labours.

JULIAN: I . . . I would have thought you'd have champagne . . . ready, that you'd be busy with the party. . . .

BUTLER: One does *many* things. You'll have your champagne, sir, never fear.

JULIAN: I'm sorry; I . . . I was so upset.

BUTLER: Yes.

JULIAN [*attempting a joke*]: After all, I've not been married before.

BUTLER: No.

JULIAN: And the procedures are a little . . . well, you know.

BUTLER: Yes.

JULIAN: . . . *still* . . .

BUTLER: Yes.

JULIAN: It all *does* seem odd.

BUTLER: Marriage is a confusing business.

JULIAN: Have . . . have you been . . . married?

[BUTLER *gives a noncommittal laugh as answer.*]

I . . . I don't know if marriage is, but certainly the circumstances surrounding this *wedding* are rather . . .

BUTLER [*a fairly chilling smile*]: Special people, special problems.

JULIAN [*hurt*]: Oh. Well . . . yes.

BUTLER [*disdainful curiosity*]: Do you . . . *feel* married?

JULIAN [*withdrawn*]: Not having been, I cannot say. [*Pause.*] Can I?

BUTLER [*takes one of the sheets, opens it with a cracking sound, holds it in front of him, a hand on each shoulder*]: No. [*Puts it to one side.*] I suppose not.

JULIAN: No. I wonder if . . . I wonder if you could go upstairs, perhaps, and see if Miss Alice . . . my *wife* . . . is . . .

BUTLER: No. [*Then, rather stern.*] I have much too much work to do. [*Cheerful.*] I'll get you some champagne, though.

JULIAN [*rather removed*]: No, I'll . . . wait for the others, if they haven't all . . . disappeared.

BUTLER [*noncommittal*]: To leave you alone with your bride, on your wedding night? No; not yet.

JULIAN [*for something to say, as much as anything, yet hopeful of an answer, or an explanation*]: Miss Alice . . . chose not to invite . . . friends . . . to the ceremony.

BUTLER [*chuckle*]: Ah, no. Alice . . . *Miss* Alice does not have friends; admirers, yes. Worshippers . . . but not buddies.

JULIAN [*puzzled*]: I asked her why she had not, and she replied . . .

BUTLER [*improvising*]: . . . it is you, Julian, who are being married . . . ?

JULIAN [*too self-absorbed to be surprised*]: Yes; something like that.

BUTLER: Your wife is . . . something of a recluse.

JULIAN [*hopeful*]: But so outgoing!

BUTLER: Yes? Well, then; you will indeed have fun. [*Mock instructions.*] Uncover the chandeliers in the ballroom! Lay on some footmen! Unplug the fountains! Trim the maze!

JULIAN [*more or less to himself*]: She *must* have friends . . . [*unsure*] must she not?

BUTLER [*stage whisper*]: I don't know; no one has ever asked her.

JULIAN [*laughing nervously*]: Oh, indeed!
   [MISS ALICE *comes hurriedly into the room; she has on a suit. She sees only* BUTLER *first.*]

MISS ALICE: Butler! Have you seen . . . ? [*Sees* JULIAN.] Oh, I'm . . . sorry. [*She begins to leave.*]

JULIAN: There you are. No, wait; wait! [*But* MISS ALICE *has left the room. In need of help.*] I find everything today puzzling.

BUTLER [*about to give advice*]: Look . . . [*Thinks better of it.*]

JULIAN: Yes?

BUTLER [*shrugs*]: Nothing. The wages of a wedding day.

JULIAN: Are you my friend?

BUTLER [*takes a while to think about the answer*]: I *am*; yes; but you'll probably think not.

JULIAN: Is something being kept from me?

BUTLER [*after a pause*]: You loathe sham, do you not?

JULIAN: Yes.

BUTLER: As do we all ... most of us. You are dedicated to the reality of things, rather than their appearance, are you not?

JULIAN: Deeply.

BUTLER: As are ... some of us.

JULIAN: It was why I retreated ... withdrew ... to the asylum.

BUTLER: Yes, yes. And you are devout.

JULIAN: You know that.

BUTLER: When you're locked in the attic, Julian, in the attic closet, in the dark, do you care who comes?

JULIAN: No. But ...

BUTLER [*starts to leave*]: Let me get the champagne.

JULIAN: Please!

BUTLER: So that we all can toast. [*As* BUTLER *leaves, the* CARDINAL *enters.*] Ah! Here comes the Church.

JULIAN [*going to the* CARDINAL, *kneeling before him, kissing his ring, holding the ring hand afterward, staying kneeling*]: Your Eminence.

CARDINAL: Julian. Our dear Julian.

BUTLER: Have you caught the bride?

CARDINAL: No. No. Not seen her since the ... since we married her.

JULIAN: It was good of you. I suspect she will be here soon. Butler, would you ... go see? If she will come here? His Eminence would ... Now do be good and go.

[BUTLER *exits.*]

He has been a great help. At times when my service has ... perplexed me, till I grew despondent, and wondered if perhaps you'd not been mistaken in putting such a burden ...

CARDINAL [*not wanting to get into it*]: Yes, yes, Julian. We have *resolved* it.

JULIAN: But then I judge it is God's doing, this . . . wrench-
ing of my life from one light to another . . .

CARDINAL: . . . Julian . . .

JULIAN: . . . though not losing God's light, joining it with
. . . my new. [*He is like a bubbling little boy.*] I can't tell
you, the . . . radiance, humming, and the witchcraft, I
think it must be, the ecstasy of this light, as *God's* exactly;
the transport the same, the lifting, the . . . the sense of
service, and the EXPANSION . . .

CARDINAL: . . . Julian . . .

JULIAN: . . . the blessed wonder of service with a renewing,
not an ending joy — that joy I thought possible only
through martyrdom, now, now the sunlight is no longer
the hope for glare and choking in the dust and plummet-
ing, but with cool and green and yellow dappled . . .
perfumes . . .

CARDINAL [*sharply*]: Julian!

JULIAN [*little-boy smile*]: Sir.

CARDINAL [*evading* JULIAN's *eyes*]: We sign the papers today, Julian. It's all arranged, the grant is accomplished;
through your marriage . . . your service.

JULIAN [*puzzlement*]: Father?

CARDINAL [*barely keeping pleasure in his voice*]: And isn't it
wonderful: that you have . . . found yourself such great
service and such . . . exceeding happiness, too; that God's
way has brought such gifts to his servant, and to his
servant's servant as well.

JULIAN [*puzzled*]: Thank you . . . Your Eminence.

CARDINAL [*sadly*]: It is your wedding day, Julian!

JULIAN [*smiles, throws off his mood*]: Yes, it is! It's my
wedding day. And a day of glory to God, that His
Church has been blessed with great wealth, for the
suffering of the world, conversion and the pronouncement
of His Glory.

CARDINAL [*embarrassed; perfunctory*]: Praise God.

JULIAN: That God has seen fit to let me be His instrument in this undertaking, that God . . .

CARDINAL: Julian. [*Pause.*] As you have accepted what has happened . . . removed, so far removed from . . . any thought . . . accept what . . . *will* happen, *may* happen, with the same humility and . . .

JULIAN [*happily*]: It is my service.

CARDINAL [*nods*]: Accept what may come . . . as God's will.

JULIAN: Don't . . . don't frighten me. Bless me, Father.

CARDINAL [*embarrassed*]: Julian, please . . .

JULIAN [*on his knees before the* CARDINAL]: Bless me?

CARDINAL [*reluctantly; appropriate gestures*]: In the name of the Father and of the Son and the Holy Ghost . . .

JULIAN: . . . Amen . . .

CARDINAL: . . . Amen. You *have* . . . confessed, Julian?

JULIAN [*blushing, but childishly pleased*]: I . . . I have, Father; I have . . . confessed, and finally, to sins more real than imagined, but . . . but they are not sins, are they, in God's name, done in God's name, Father?

CARDINAL: May the presence of our Lord, Jesus Christ be with you always . . .

JULIAN: . . . to . . . to shield my eyes from too much light, that I may be always worthy . . .

CARDINAL: . . . to light your way for you in the darkness . . .

JULIAN: . . . dark, darkness, Father? . . .

CARDINAL: . . . that you may be worthy of whatever sacrifice, unto death itself . . .

JULIAN: . . . in all this light! . . .

CARDINAL: . . . is asked of you; that you may accept what you do not understand . . .

JULIAN [*a mild argument*]: But, Father . . .

CARDINAL: . . . and that the Lord may have mercy on your soul . . . as, indeed, may He have on us all . . . all our souls.

JULIAN: . . . A . . . Amen?

CARDINAL [*nodding*]: Amen.

LAWYER [*entering*]: Well, well. Your Eminence. Julian.
Well, you are indeed a fortunate man, today. What more
cheering sight can there be than Frank Fearnought,
clean-living, healthy farm lad, come from the heartland
of the country, from the asylums – you see, I know –
in search of fame, and true love – never fortune, of
course.

JULIAN: . . . Please . . .

LAWYER: And see what has happened to brave and handsome Frank: he has found what he sought . . . true . . .
love; *and* fortune – to his surprise, for wealth had never
crossed his pure mind; and fame? . . . Oooooh, there will
be a private fame, perhaps.

CARDINAL: *Very* pretty.

LAWYER: And we are dressed in city ways, too, are we not?
No longer the simple gown of the farm lad, the hems
trailing in the dung; no; now we are in city clothes . . .
banker's clothes.

JULIAN: These are proper clothes.

LAWYER: As you will discover, poor priestlet, poor former
priestlet. Dressed differently for the sacrifice, eh?

JULIAN: I . . . think I'll . . . look for Miss . . . for my wife.

LAWYER: Do.

CARDINAL: Oh, yes, Julian; please.

JULIAN [*kneels, kisses the ring again*]: Your Eminence. [*To
the* LAWYER, *mildly.*] We are both far too old . . . are we
not . . . for all that?

   [JULIAN *exits.*]

CARDINAL [*after* JULIAN *leaves*]: Is cruelty a lesson you
learned at your mother's knee? One of the songs you
were taught?

LAWYER: One learns by growing, as they say. I have fine
instructors behind me . . . yourself amongst them. [*A
dismissing gesture.*] We have no time. [*Raises his briefcase,*

then throws it on a table.] All here. [*Great cheerfulness.*] All here! The grant: all your money. [*Normal tone again.*] I must say, your Church lawyers are picky men.

CARDINAL: Thorough.

LAWYER: Picky. Humourless on small matters, great wits on the major ones; ribald over the whole proposition.

CARDINAL [*mumbling*]: . . . hardly a subject for ribaldry . . .

LAWYER: Oh, quite a dowry, greatest marriage settlement in history, *mother* church indeed . . . things like that.

CARDINAL [*unhappily*]: Well, it's all over now . . .

LAWYER: Almost.

CARDINAL: Yes.

LAWYER: Cheer up; the price was high enough.

CARDINAL: Then it is . . . really true? About . . . *this*? [*Points at the model.*]

LAWYER: I haven't time to lie to you.

CARDINAL: Really . . . true.

LAWYER [*moving to the model*]: Really. Can't you accept the wonders of the world? Why not of this one, as well as the other?

CARDINAL: We should be . . . getting on.

LAWYER: Yes. [*Points to a place in the model.*] Since the wedding was . . . *here* . . . and we are [*indicates the room they are in*] here . . . we have come quite a . . . dimension, have we not?

[*The* LAWYER *moves away from the model to a table, as the* CARDINAL *stays at the model.*]

CARDINAL [*abstracted*]: Yes. A distance. [*Turns, sees the* LAWYER *open a drawer, take out a pistol and check its cartridges.*] What . . . what are you doing? [*Moves toward the* LAWYER, *slowly.*]

LAWYER: House pistol.

CARDINAL: But what are you doing?

LAWYER [*looking it over carefully*]: I've never shot one of these things . . . pistols. [*Then, to answer.*] I'm looking at it . . . to be sure the cartridges are there, to see that it is oiled, or whatever is done to it . . . to see how it functions.

CARDINAL: But . . .

LAWYER [*calmly*]: You know we may have to shoot him; you know that may be necessary.

CARDINAL [*sadly and softly*]: Dear God, no.

LAWYER [*looking at the gun*]: I suppose all you do is . . . pull. [*Looks at the* CARDINAL.] If the great machinery threatens . . . to come to a halt . . . the great axis on which all turns . . . if it needs oil . . . well, we lubricate it, do we not? And if blood is the only oil handy . . . what is a little blood?

CARDINAL [*false bravura*]: But that will not be necessary. [*Great empty quiet loss.*] Dear God, let that not be necessary.

LAWYER: Better off dead, perhaps. You know? Eh?

CARDINAL: The making of a martyr? A saint?

LAWYER: Well, let's make that saint when we come to him.

CARDINAL: Dear God, let that not be necessary.

LAWYER: Why not? Give me *any* person . . . a martyr, if you wish . . . a saint . . . He'll take what he gets for . . . what he wishes it to be. AH, it is what I have always wanted, he'll say, looking terror and betrayal straight in the eye. Why not: face the inevitable and call it what you have always wanted. How to come out on top, going under.

[JULIAN *enters.*]

LAWYER: Ah! There you are. Still not with Miss Alice!

JULIAN: I seem not to be with anyone.

LAWYER [*smile*]: Isn't that odd?

JULIAN [*turning away, more to himself*]: I would have thought it so.

CARDINAL [*hearty, but ill at ease*]: One would have thought to have it all now – corks popping, glasses splintering in the fireplace . . .

LAWYER: When Christ told Peter – so legends tell – that

he would found his church upon that rock, He must have had in mind an island in a sea of wine. How firm a foundation in the vintage years . . .

[*We hear voices from without; they do, too.*]

MISS ALICE [*offstage*]: I don't *want* to go in there . . .

BUTLER [*offstage*]: You *have* to come in, now . . .

MISS ALICE [*offstage*]: I won't go *in* there . . .

BUTLER [*offstage*]: Come along now; don't be a child . . .

MISS ALICE [*offstage*]: I . . . won't . . . *go* . . .

[BUTLER *appears; two champagne bottles in one hand, pulling* MISS ALICE *with the other.*]

BUTLER: Come along!

MISS ALICE [*as she enters; sotto voce*]: I don't want to . . . [*As she sees the others see her, she stops talking, smiles, tries to save the entrance.*]

BUTLER: Lurking in the gallery, talking to the ancestral wall, but I found her.

MISS ALICE: Don't be silly; I was . . . [*Shrugs.*]

BUTLER [*shrugs, too*] : Suit yourself. Champagne, everybody!

JULIAN: Ah! Good. [*Moving toward* MISS ALICE.] Are you all right?

MISS ALICE [*moves away from him; rather impatiently*]: Yes.

CARDINAL: But you've changed your clothes, and your wedding gown was . . .

MISS ALICE: . . . two hundred years old . . .

LAWYER: . . . fragile.

CARDINAL: Ah!

[*Something of a silence falls. The other characters are away from* JULIAN; *unless otherwise specified, they will keep a distance, surrounding him, but more than at arm's length. They will observe him, rather clinically, and while this shift of attitude must be subtle, it must also be evident.* JULIAN *will grow to knowledge of it, will aid us, though we will be aware of it before he is.*]

JULIAN [*to break the silence*]: Well, shall we have the champagne?

BUTLER: Stay there! [*Pause.*] I'll bring it.

CARDINAL: Once, when we were in France, we toured the champagne country . . .

LAWYER [*no interest*]: Really.

CARDINAL: Saw the . . . mechanics, so to speak, of how it was done . . .

LAWYER: Peasants? Treading?

CARDINAL [*laughs*]: No, no. That is for woodcuts.

[*The cork pops.*]

Ah!

BUTLER: Nobody move! I'll bring it to you all. [*Starts pouring into glasses already placed to the side.*]

MISS ALICE [*to the* LAWYER]: The ceremony.

[*He does not reply.*]

The ceremony!

LAWYER [*overly sweet smile*]: Yes. [*To them all.*] The ceremony.

CARDINAL: Another? Must we officiate?

LAWYER: No need.

JULIAN [*a little apprehensive*]: What . . . ceremony is this?

BUTLER [*his back to them*]: There's never as much in a champagne bottle as I expect there to be; I never learn. Or, perhaps the glasses are larger than they seem.

LAWYER [*ironic*]: When the lights go on all over the world . . . the true world. The ceremony of Alice.

JULIAN [*to* MISS ALICE]: What is this about?

[*She nods toward the* LAWYER.]

LAWYER: Butler? Are you poured?

BUTLER [*finishing; squeezing the bottle*]: Yeeeeesssss . . .

LAWYER: Pass.

BUTLER [*starts passing the tray of glasses*]: Miss Alice.

MISS ALICE [*strained*]: Thank you.

BUTLER [*starts toward* JULIAN, *changes his mind, goes to the* CARDINAL]: Your Eminence?

CARDINAL: Ahhh.

BUTLER [*starts toward* JULIAN *again, changes his mind, goes to the* LAWYER]: Sweetheart?

LAWYER: Thank you.

BUTLER [*finally goes to* JULIAN, *holds the tray at arm's length; speaks, not unkindly*]: Our Brother Julian.

JULIAN [*shy friendliness*]: Thank you, Butler.

LAWYER: And now . . .

BUTLER [*moving back to the table with the tray*]: Hold on; I haven't got mine yet. It's over here.

JULIAN: Yes! Butler must drink with us. [*To* MISS ALICE.] Don't you think so?

MISS ALICE [*curiously weary*]: Why not? He's family.

LAWYER [*moving toward the model*]: Yes; what a large family you have.

[*The* LAWYER *would naturally have to pass near* JULIAN; *pauses, detours.*]

JULIAN: I'm sorry; am . . . am I in your way?

LAWYER [*continues to the model*]: Large family, years of adding. The ceremony, children. The ceremony of Alice. [*The others have turned, are facing the model. The* LAWYER *raises his glass.*] To Julian and his bride.

CARDINAL: Hear, hear.

JULIAN [*blushing*]: Oh, my goodness.

LAWYER: To Julian and his bride; to Alice's wisdom, wealth and whatever.

BUTLER [*quietly, seriously*]: To Alice.

MISS ALICE: To Alice.

[*Brief pause; only* JULIAN *turns his head, is about to speak, but . . .*]

LAWYER: To their marriage. To their binding together, acceptance and worship . . . received; accepted.

BUTLER: To Alice.

LAWYER: To the marriage vow between them, which has brought joy to them both, and great benefit to the Church.

CARDINAL: Amen.

MISS ALICE: To Alice.

[*Again only* JULIAN *responds to this; a half turn of the head.*]

LAWYER: To their house.

BUTLER, MISS ALICE and CARDINAL [*not quite together*]: To their house.

JULIAN [*after them*]: To their house.

LAWYER: To the chapel wherein they were bound in wedlock.

[*A light goes on in a room in the model.* JULIAN *makes sounds of amazement; the others are silent.*]

To their quarters.

[*Light goes on upstairs in the model.*]

To the private rooms where marriage lives.

BUTLER: To Alice.

MISS ALICE: To Alice.

[*To which* JULIAN *does not respond this time.*]

LAWYER: And to this room . . .

[*Another light goes on in the model.*]

. in which they are met, in which we are met . . . to celebrate their coming together.

BUTLER: Amen.

LAWYER: A union whose spiritual values shall be uppermost . . .

MISS ALICE: That's enough. . . .

LAWYER: . . . whose carnal side shall . . .

MISS ALICE: That's enough!

JULIAN: May . . . May I! [*It is important that he stay facing the model, not* MISS ALICE. BUTLER, *who is behind him, may look at him; the* CARDINAL *will look to the floor.*] May I . . . propose. To the wonders . . . which may befall a man . . .

least where he is looking, least that he would have
thought; to the clear plan of that which we call chance,
to what we see as accident till our humility returns to us
when we are faced with the mysteries. To all that which
we really want, until our guile and pride . . .

CARDINAL [*still looking at the floor*]: . . . Julian . . .

JULIAN: . . . betray us? [*Looks at the* CARDINAL; *pauses,
goes on, smiling sweetly.*] My gratitude . . . my wonder . . .
and my love.

LAWYER [*pause*]: Amen?

JULIAN: Amen.

LAWYER [*abruptly turning*]: Then, if we're packed, let us go.

BUTLER [*not moving*]: Dust covers.

JULIAN [*still smiling*]: Go?

CARDINAL [*to delay*]: Well. *This* champagne glass seems
smaller than one would have guessed; it has emptied
itself . . . on one toast!

LAWYER: I recall. Suddenly I recall it. When we were
children. [*Quite fascinated with what he is saying.*] When we
were children and we would gather in the dark, two of
us . . . any two . . . on a swing, side porch, or by the
ocean, sitting backed against a boulder, and we would
explore . . . those most private parts, of one another, any
two of us . . . [*shrugs*] boy, girl, how – when we did it – we
would talk of other things . . . of our schoolwork, or
where we would travel in the summer. How, as our
shaking hands passed under skirts or undid buttons,
sliding, how we would, both of us, talk of other things,
whispering, our voices shaking as our just barely moving
hands. [*Laughs, points to the* CARDINAL.] Like you!
Chattering there on the model! Your mind on us and
what is happening. Oh, the subterfuges.

MISS ALICE: I am packed.

JULIAN [*still off by himself*]: Packed? . . . Miss Alice?

MISS ALICE [*to the* LAWYER; *cold*]: May we leave soon?

JULIAN: Miss . . . Alice?

MISS ALICE: May we?

LAWYER [*pause*]: Fairly.

JULIAN [*sharp*]: Miss Alice!

MISS ALICE [*turns toward him; flat tone; a recitation*]: I'm very happy for you, Julian, you've done well.

JULIAN [*backing away from everyone a little*]: What is . . . going on . . . here? [*To* MISS ALICE.] Tell me!

MISS ALICE [*as if she is not interested*]: I am packed. We are going.

JULIAN [*sudden understanding*]: Ah! [*Points to himself.*] *We* are going. But where? You . . . didn't tell me we . . . we were . . .

MISS ALICE [*to the* LAWYER, *moving away*]: Tell him.

JULIAN: . . . going somewhere. . . .

MISS ALICE [*quite furious*]: Tell him!

LAWYER [*about to make a speech*]: Brother Julian . . .

JULIAN [*strained*]: I am no longer Brother.

LAWYER [*oily*]: Oh, are we not all brothers?

JULIAN [*to* MISS ALICE; *with a halfhearted gesture*]: Come stand by me.

MISS ALICE [*surprisingly little-girl fright*]: No!

LAWYER: Now. Julian.

CARDINAL: Order yourself, Julian.

JULIAN [*to the* CARDINAL]: Sir?

LAWYER [*sarcasm is gone; all is gone, save fact*]: Dear Julian; we all serve, do we not? Each of us his own priesthood; publicly, some, others . . . within only; but we all do – what's-his-name's special trumpet, or clear lonely bell. Predestination, fate, the will of God, accident . . . All swirled up in it, no matter what the name. And being man, we have invented choice, and have, indeed, gone further, and have catalogued the underpinnings of choice. But we do not know. Anything. End prologue.

MISS ALICE: Tell him.

LAWYER: No matter. We are leaving you now, Julian; agents, every one of us – going. We are leaving you ... to your accomplishment: your marriage, your wife, your ... special priesthood.

JULIAN [*apprehension and great suspicion*]: I ... don't know what you're talking about.

LAWYER [*unperturbed*]: What is so amazing is the ... coming together ... of disparates ... left-fielding, out of the most unlikely. Who would have thought, Julian? Who would have thought? You have brought us to the end of our service here. We go on; you stay.

BUTLER: May I begin to cover?

MISS ALICE: Not yet. [*Kindly.*] Do you understand, Julian?

JULIAN [*barely in control*]: Of course not!

MISS ALICE: Julian, I have tried to be ... *her*. No; I have tried to be ... what I thought she might, what might make you happy, what you might use, as a ... what?

BUTLER: *Play* God; go on.

MISS ALICE: We must ... represent, draw pictures, reduce or enlarge to ... to what we can understand.

JULIAN [*sad, mild*]: But I have fought against it ... all my life. When they said, 'Bring the wonders down to me, closer; I cannot see them, touch; nor can I believe.' I have fought against it ... all my life.

BUTLER [*to* MISS ALICE; *softly*]: You see? No good.

MISS ALICE [*shrugs*]: I have done what I can with it.

JULIAN: All my life. In and out of ... confinement, fought against the symbol.

MISS ALICE: Then you should be happy now.

CARDINAL: Julian, it has been your desire always to serve; your sense of mission ...

LAWYER: We are surrogates; *our* task is done now.

MISS ALICE: Stay with her.

JULIAN [*horror behind it; disbelieving*]: Stay ... with ... her?

MISS ALICE: Stay with her. Accept it.

LAWYER [*at the model*]: Her rooms are lighted. It is warm, there is enough.

MISS ALICE: Be content with it. Stay with her.

JULIAN [*refusing to accept what he is hearing*]: Miss Alice . . . I have married *you*.

MISS ALICE [*kind, still*]: No, Julian; you have married *her* . . . through me.

JULIAN [*pointing to the model*]: There is nothing there! We are *here*! There is no one *there*!

LAWYER: *She* is there . . . we believe.

JULIAN [*to* MISS ALICE]: I have *been* with *you*!

MISS ALICE [*not explaining; sort of dreamy*]: You have felt her warmth through me, touched her lips through my lips, held hands, through mine, my breasts, hers, lain on her bed, through mine, wrapped yourself in her wings, your hands on the small of her back, your mouth on her hair, the voice in your ear, hers not mine, all hers; her. You are hers.

CARDINAL: Accept.

BUTLER: Accept.

LAWYER: Accept.

JULIAN: THERE IS NO ONE THERE!

MISS ALICE: She is there.

JULIAN [*rushes to the model, shouts at it*]: THERE IS NOTHING THERE! [*Turns to them all.*] THERE IS NOTHING THERE!

CARDINAL [*softly*]: Accept it, Julian.

JULIAN [*all the power he has*]: ACCEPT IT!

LAWYER [*quietly*]: All legal, all accomplished, all satisfied, that which we believe.

JULIAN: ACCEPT!

BUTLER: . . . that which is done, and may not be revoked.

CARDINAL [*with some difficulty*]: . . . yes.

JULIAN: WHAT AM I TO ACCEPT?

LAWYER: An act of faith.

JULIAN [*slow, incredulous*]: An . . . act . . . of . . . faith!

LAWYER [*snaps his fingers at the* CARDINAL]: Buddy?

CARDINAL: Uh . . . yes, Julian, an . . . act of faith, indeed. It is . . . believed.

LAWYER [*deadly serious, but with a small smile*]: Yes, it is . . . believed. It is what we believe, therefore what we know. Is that not right? Faith is knowledge?

CARDINAL: An act of faith, Julian, however we must . . .

JULIAN [*horror*]: FAITH!?

CARDINAL: . . . in God's will . . .

JULIAN: GOD'S! WILL!

CARDINAL [*as if his ears are hurting, sort of mumbling*]: Yes, Julian, you see, we must accept, and . . . be glad, yes, be glad . . . our ecstasy.

JULIAN [*backing off a little, shaking his head*]: I have not come this distance . . .

CARDINAL [*moving toward him a little*]: Julian . . .

JULIAN: Stay back! I have not come this long way . . . have not – in all sweet obedience – walked in these . . . [*realizes he is differently dressed*] those robes . . . to be MOCKED.

LAWYER: Accept it, Julian.

JULIAN: I have not come this long *way*!

BUTLER: Yes; oh, yes.

JULIAN: I HAVE NOT!

MISS ALICE [*kindly*]: Julian . . . dear Julian; accept.

JULIAN [*turns toward her, supplicating*]: I have not worn and given up for . . . for mockery; I have not stretched out the path of my life before me, to walk on straight, to be . . .

MISS ALICE: Accept.

JULIAN: I have not fought the nightmares – and the waking demons, yes – and the years of despair, those, too . . . I have not accepted *half*, for *nothing*.

CARDINAL: For everything.

MISS ALICE: Dear Julian; accept. Allow us all to rest.

JULIAN [*a child's terror of being alone*]: NO!

MISS ALICE [*still kind*]: You must.

BUTLER: No choice.

JULIAN: I have . . . have . . . given up everything to gain everything, for the sake of my faith and my peace; I have allowed and followed, and sworn and cherished, but I have *not*, have *not* . . .

MISS ALICE: Be with her. Please.

JULIAN: For halluci*nation*? I HAVE DONE WITH HALLU-CINATION.

MISS ALICE: Then have done with forgery, Julian; accept what's real. I am the . . . illusion.

JULIAN [*retreating*]: No . . . no no no, oh no.

LAWYER [*quietly*]: All legal, all accomplished, all satisfied, that which we believe.

MISS ALICE: All done.

JULIAN [*quite frightened*]: I . . . choose . . . *not*.

CARDINAL: There is no choice here, Julian. . . .

LAWYER: No choice at all.

MISS ALICE [*hands apart*]: All done.

[JULIAN *begins backing toward the model; the* LAWYER *begins crossing to the desk wherein he has put the gun.*]

BUTLER [*quietly*]: I *must* cover now; the cars are waiting.

JULIAN: No . . . no . . . I WILL NOT ACCEPT THIS.

LAWYER [*snaps for the* CARDINAL *again*]: Buddy . . .

CARDINAL: We . . . [*Harder tone.*] I *order* you.

LAWYER [*smile*]: There. Now will you accept?

JULIAN: I . . . cannot be so mistaken, to have . . . I cannot have so misunderstood my life; I cannot have . . . was I sane *then*? Those *years*? My time in the *asylum*? WAS THAT WHEN I WAS RATIONAL? THEN?

CARDINAL: Julian . . .

LAWYER [*taking the gun from the drawer, checking it; to the* CARDINAL]: Don't you teach your people anything? Do you let them improvise? *Make* their Gods? *Make* them as they *see* them?

JULIAN [*rage in the terror*]: I HAVE ACCEPTED GOD.

LAWYER [*turns to* JULIAN, *gun in hand*]: Then accept his works. Resign yourself to the mysteries . . .

MISS ALICE: . . . to greater wisdom.

LAWYER: Take it! Accept what you're given.

MISS ALICE: Your priesthood, Julian – full, at last. Stay with her. Accept your service.

JULIAN: I . . . cannot . . . accept . . . this.

LAWYER [*aims*]: Very well, then.

JULIAN: I have not come this . . . given up so much for . . .

BUTLER: Accept it, Julian.

MISS ALICE: Stay with her.

JULIAN: No, no, I will . . . I will go *back*! I will . . . go *back* to it. [*Starts backing toward the stairs.*] To . . . to . . . I will go back to the asylum.

LAWYER: Last chance.

MISS ALICE: Accept it, Julian.

JULIAN: To . . . my asylum. MY! ASYLUM! My . . . my refuge . . . in the world, from all the demons waking, my . . . REFUGE!

LAWYER: Very well then.

> [*Shoots. Then silence.* JULIAN *does not cry out, but clutches his belly, stumbles forward a few steps, sinks to the floor in front of the model.*]

MISS ALICE [*softly, with compassion*]: Oh, Julian. [*To the* LAWYER; *calm.*] He would have stayed.

LAWYER [*to* MISS ALICE, *shrugging*]: It was an accident.

JULIAN: Fa . . . ther?

MISS ALICE: Poor Julian. [*To the* LAWYER.] You did not have to do that; I could have made him stay.

LAWYER: Perhaps. But what does it matter . . . one man . . . in the face of so much.

JULIAN: Fa . . . ther?

BUTLER [*going to* JULIAN]: Let me look.

MISS ALICE [*starting to go to him*]: Oh, poor Julian . . .

LAWYER [*stopping her*]: Stay where you are.
> [BUTLER *goes to* JULIAN *while the others keep their places.*
> BUTLER *bends over him, maybe pulling his head back.*]

BUTLER: Do you want a doctor for him?

LAWYER [*after a tiny pause*]: Why?

BUTLER [*straightening up*]: Because . . .

LAWYER: Yes?

BUTLER [*quite matter-of-fact*]: Because he will bleed to death without attention?

JULIAN [*to the* CARDINAL]: Help . . . me?
> [*In answer, the* CARDINAL *looks back to the* LAWYER, *asking a question with his silence.*]

LAWYER [*after a pause*]: No doctor.

BUTLER [*moving away*]: No doctor.

MISS ALICE [*to the* LAWYER; *great sadness*]: No?

LAWYER [*some compassion*]: No.

JULIAN: Father!

CARDINAL [*anguished*]: Please, Julian.

JULIAN [*anger through the pain*]: In the sight of God? You dare?

LAWYER: Or in the sight of man. He dares. [*Moves to the table, putting the gun away, taking up the briefcase.*]

JULIAN [*again*]: You dare!?
> [BUTLER *goes to cover something.*]

LAWYER [*taking the briefcase to the* CARDINAL]: There it is, all of it. All legal now, the total grant: two billion, kid, twenty years of grace for no work at all; no labour . . . at least not yours. [*Holds the briefcase out.*] There . . . take it.

CARDINAL: We do not . . . fetch and carry. And have not acquiesced . . . [*Indicates briefcase.*] For *this*.

JULIAN [*weak again*]: Father?

LAWYER: Not God's errand boy?

CARDINAL: God's; not yours.

LAWYER: *Who* are the Gods?

JULIAN [*pain*]: God in heaven!

MISS ALICE: Poor Julian! [*Goes to him; they create something of a Pietà.*] Rest back; lean on me.

LAWYER [*withdrawing his offer of the briefcase*]: Perhaps your *new* secretary can pick it up. You *will* go on, won't you – red gown and amethyst, until the pelvic cancer comes, or the coronary blacks it out, all of it? The good with it, and the evil? [*Indicates* JULIAN.] Even this? In the final mercy?

    [*The* CARDINAL *looks straight ahead of him for a moment, hesitates, then walks out, looking neither left nor right.*]

BUTLER [*calling after him, halfhearted and intentionally too late*]: Any of the cars will do . . . [*trailing off*] . . . as they're all hired.

JULIAN: Who . . . who left? Who!

MISS ALICE [*comforting him*]: You're shivering, Julian . . . *so*.

JULIAN [*almost a laugh*]: Am I?

LAWYER [*still looking after the departed* CARDINAL]: Once, when I was at school – our departed reminds me – once, when I was at school, I was writing poetry – well, no, poems, which were published in the literary magazine. And each issue a teacher from the English Department would criticize the work in the school newspaper a week or two hence.

MISS ALICE [*to* JULIAN]: A blanket?

JULIAN: No. Hold close.

LAWYER: And one teacher, who was a wag and was, as well, a former student, wrote of one of my poems – a sonnet, as I recall – that it had all the grace of a walking crow.

MISS ALICE [*ibid.*]: I don't want to hurt.

JULIAN: Closer . . . please. Warmth.

LAWYER: I was green in those years, and, besides, I could not recall how crows walked.

MISS ALICE [*ibid.*]: How like a little boy you are.

JULIAN: I'm lonely.

LAWYER: Could not recall that I had ever *seen* a crow . . . walking.

MISS ALICE: Is being afraid always the same – no matter the circumstances, the age?

JULIAN: It is the attic room, always; the closet. Hold close.

LAWYER [*fully aware of the counterpoint by now, aiding it*]: And so I went to see him – the wag – about the walking crow . . . the poem, actually.

BUTLER [*putting a cover on something*]: Crows don't walk much . . .

JULIAN: . . . and it is very dark; always. And no one will come . . . for the longest time.

MISS ALICE: Yes.

LAWYER: Yes; that is what he said – sitting with his back against all the books, 'Crows don't walk much . . . if they can help it . . . if they can fly.'

JULIAN: No. No one will come.

BUTLER [*snapping open a cover*]: *I* could have told you that; surprised you didn't know it. Crows walk around a lot only when they're sick.

LAWYER: 'Santayanian finesse.'

JULIAN: No one will come . . . for the longest time; if ever.

MISS ALICE [*agreeing*]: No.

LAWYER: That was the particular thing: 'Santayanian finesse.' He said that had . . . all the grace of a walking crow.

BUTLER [*rubbing something for dust*]: Bright man.

LAWYER [*to* BUTLER]: I don't know; he stayed on some years after I left – after our walking bird and I left – then went on to some other school. . . . [*To* MISS ALICE, *immediately*.] Are you ready to go?

MISS ALICE [*looking up; sad irony*]: Am I ready to go on with it, do you mean? To move to the city now before the train trip south? The private car? The house on the ocean, the ... same mysteries, the evasions, the perfect plotting? The removed residence, the Rolls twice weekly into the shopping strip ... all of it?

LAWYER: Yes. All of it.

MISS ALICE [*looks to* JULIAN, *considers a moment*]: Are you warm now?

JULIAN: Yes ... and cold.

MISS ALICE [*looks up to the* LAWYER, *smiles faintly*]: No.

LAWYER: Then get up and come along.

MISS ALICE [*to the* LAWYER]: And all the rest of it?

LAWYER: Yes.

MISS ALICE: The years of it ... to go on? For how long?

LAWYER: Until we are replaced.

MISS ALICE [*with a tiny, tinkling laugh*]: Oh God.

LAWYER: Or until everything is desert [*shrugs*] ... on the chance that *it* runs out before *we* do.

BUTLER [*examining the phrenological head*]: I have never even examined phrenology.

LAWYER: But more likely till we are replaced.

JULIAN [*with a sort of quiet wonder*]: I am cold at the core ... where it burns most.

MISS ALICE [*sad truth*]: Yes. [*Then to the* LAWYER.] Yes.

LAWYER [*almost affectionately*]: So, come now; gather yourself.

MISS ALICE [*restrained pleading*]: But, he is still ... ill ...

JULIAN [*to* MISS ALICE, *probably, but not at* her]: You wish to go away now?

MISS ALICE [*to the* LAWYER]: You see how he takes to me? You see how it *is* natural? Poor Julian.

LAWYER: Let's go.

MISS ALICE [*to* JULIAN]: I *must* go away from you now; it is not that I wish to. [*To* BUTLER.] Butler, I have left my wig, it is upstairs ...

BUTLER [*rather testy*]: I'm sorry, I'm covering, I'm busy.

LAWYER [*turning to go*]: Let me; it's such a pretty wig,

becomes you so. And there are one or two other things I'd like to check.

MISS ALICE [*sad smile*]: The pillowcases? Put your ear against them? To eavesdrop? Or the sheets? To see if they're still writhing?

[*The* LAWYER *almost says something, thinks better of it, exits.*]

Poor Julian.

BUTLER: Then we all are to be together.

MISS ALICE [*small laugh*]: Oh God, you heard him: forever.

BUTLER: I like it where it's warm.

MISS ALICE: I dreaded once, when I was in my teens, that I would grow old, look back, over the precipice, and discover that I had not lived my life. [*Short abrupt laugh.*] Oh Lord!

JULIAN [*now a semi-coma, almost sweet*]: How long wilt thou forget me, O Lord? Forever?

BUTLER: We live *something*.

MISS ALICE: Yes.

JULIAN: How long wilt thou hide thy face from me?

BUTLER [*to* JULIAN]: Psalm Thirteen.

MISS ALICE [*to* JULIAN]: Yes?

JULIAN: Yes.

BUTLER: How long shall my enemy be exalted over me?

JULIAN: Yes.

MISS ALICE: Not long.

BUTLER [*looking at a cover*]: Consider and hear me, O Lord, my God.

JULIAN: What does it mean if the pain . . . ebbs?

BUTLER [*considered; kindly*]: It means the agony is less.

MISS ALICE: Yes.

JULIAN [*rueful laugh*]: Consciousness, then, is pain. [*Looks up at* MISS ALICE.] All disappointments, all treacheries. [*Ironic laugh.*] Oh, God.

BUTLER: Why are we taking separate cars, then?

MISS ALICE: Well, I might ride rubbing hips on either side with a different lover, bouncing along, but ... Alice, Miss Alice would not. [*Pause.*] Would I? I would not do that. She.

BUTLER: I love you ... not her. Or ... quite differently.

MISS ALICE: Shhhh ...

BUTLER: For ages, *I* look at the sheets, listen to the pillowcases, when they're brought down, sidle into the laundry room ...

MISS ALICE: Don't.

[JULIAN *makes a sound of great pain.*]
Oh! ... Oh! ...

JULIAN [*commenting on the pain*]: Dear ... God ... in ... heaven ...

MISS ALICE: Calm; be calm now.

BUTLER [*wistful*]: But you pass through everyone, everything ... touching just briefly, lightly, passing.

MISS ALICE: My poor Julian. [*To the model.*] Receive him? Take him in?

JULIAN [*a little boy, scared*]: Who are you talking to?

MISS ALICE [*breathing it*]: Alice ...

JULIAN: Alice? Ah.

BUTLER: Will we be coming back ... when the weather changes?

MISS ALICE [*triste*]: Probably.

JULIAN [*confirming the previous exchange*]: Alice?

MISS ALICE: Yes.

JULIAN: Ah.

BUTLER [*understanding what he has been told*]: Ah.

[*The* LAWYER *enters with* MISS ALICE's *wig.*]

LAWYER: Bed stripped, mothballs lying on it like hailstones; no sound, movement, nothing. [*Puts the wig on the phrenological head.*] Do you want company, Julian? Do you want a friend? [*To* MISS ALICE.] Looks nice there. Leave it; we'll get you another. Are you ready to go?

MISS ALICE [*weary*]: You want me to go now?

LAWYER [*correcting her*]: Come.

MISS ALICE: Yes. [*Begins to disengage herself.*] Butler, come help me; we can't leave Julian just . . .

BUTLER: Yes. [*Moves to help her.*]

JULIAN [*as they take him by the arm*]: Don't do that!

MISS ALICE: Julian, we must move you . . .

JULIAN: Don't.

LAWYER [*without emotion*]: Leave him where he is.

JULIAN: Leave me . . . be. [*He slides along the floor, backing up against the model.*] Leave me . . . where I am.

LAWYER: Good pose: leave him there.

BUTLER [*getting a chair cushion*]: Cushion.

JULIAN: All . . . hurts.

BUTLER [*putting the cushion behind him*]: Easy . . .

JULIAN: ALL HURTS!!

MISS ALICE [*coming to him*]: Oh, my poor Julian . . .

JULIAN [*surprisingly strong, angry*]: LEAVE ME!

 [MISS ALICE *considers a moment, turns, leaves.*]

LAWYER [*walks over to* JULIAN, *regards him; almost casually*]: Goodbye.

JULIAN [*softly, but a malediction*]: Instrument!

LAWYER [*turns on his heel, walks out, saying as he goes*]: Butler? [*Exits.*]

BUTLER [*as* LAWYER *goes; abstracted*]: Yes . . . dear.

JULIAN [*half laughed, pained incredulity*]: Good . . . bye!

BUTLER [*looks about the room*]: All in order, I think.

JULIAN [*wistful*]: Help me?

BUTLER: My work done.

JULIAN: No?

 [BUTLER *regards* JULIAN *for a moment, then walks over, bends, kisses* JULIAN *on the forehead, not a quick kiss.*]

BUTLER: Goodbye, dear Julian. [*As* BUTLER *exits, he closes the doors behind him.*]

JULIAN [*alone, for a moment, then, whispered*]: Goodbye, dear

Julian. [*Pause.*] Exit . . . all. [*Softly.*] Help me . . . come
back, help me. [*Pause.*] HELP ME! [*Pause.*] No . . . no help.
Kiss. A kiss goodbye, from . . . whom? . . . Oh. From,
from one . . . an . . . arms: around me; warming. COME
BACK AND HELP ME. [*Pause.*] If only to stay *with* me,
while it . . . *if* . . . while it happens. For . . . you, you
would not have left me if it . . . were not . . . would you?
No. [*Calling to them.*] I HAVE NEVER DREAMED OF IT.
NEVER . . . IMAGINED . . . [*To himself again.*] what it
would be like. [*As if they were near the door.*] I died once,
when I was little . . . almost, running, fell past jagged
iron, noticed . . . only when I . . . tried to get up, that my
leg, left, was torn . . . the whole thigh *and* calf . . . down.
Such . . . *searing* . . . pain? Sweet smell of blood, screaming at the sight of it, so *far* . . . away from the house, and
in the field, all hot . . . and yellow, white in the sun.
COME BACK TO ME. Sunday, and my parents off . . .
somewhere, only my grandfather, and he . . . OFF:
SOMEWHERE: mousing with the dog. All the way down
. . . bone, flesh, meat, moving. Help me, Grandfather!
'Ere I die, ere life ebbs.' [*Laughs softly.*] Oh, Christ.
[*Little boy.*] Grandfather? Mousing? Come to me: Julian
bleeds, leg torn, from short pants to shoe, bone, meat open
to the sun; come to him. [*Looks at the model, above and
behind him.*] Ahhhh. Will no one come? [*Looks at the ceiling.*] High; high walls . . . summit. [*Eyes on his leg.*] Belly
. . . not leg. Come, grandfather! Not leg, belly! Double-
button. Pinpoint, searing . . . pain? 'If you . . . if you die.'
Are you sleeping, not mousing? Sleeping on the sun-
porch? Hammocking? Yes. 'If I die before *you* wake, will
the Lord deign *your* soul take?' Grandfather? [*Cry of pain,
then.*] Oh . . . GOD! 'I come to thee, in agony.' [*Cry to the
void.*] HELP . . . ME! [*Pause.*] No help. Stitch it up like a
wineskin! Hold the wine in. Stitch it up. [*Sweet reminis-
cence.*] And every day, put him in the sun, quarter over,

for the whole stitched leg . . . to bake, in the healing sun. Green? Yes, a little, but that's the medicine. And keep him out of the fields, chuckle, chuckle. And every day, swinging in the sun, baking; good. Aching all the while, but good. The cat comes, sniffs it, won't stay. Finally . . . stays; lies in the bend, doubling it, purring, breathing, soaking in the sun, as the leg throbs, aches, heals. 'How will I know thee, O Lord, when I am in thy sight? How will I know thee?' By my *faith*. Ah, I see. [*Furious, shouting at the roof.*] BY FAITH? THE FAITH I HAVE SHOWN THEE? BENT MYSELF? What may we avoid! Not birth! Growing up? Yes. Maturing? Oh, *God*! Growing old, and? . . . yes, growing old; but not the last; merely when. [*Sweet singsong.*] But to live again, be born once more, sure in the sight of . . . [*Shouts again.*] THERE IS NO ONE! [*Turns his head toward the closed doors, sadly.*] Unless you are listening there. Unless you have left me, tiptoed off some, stood whispering, smothered giggles, and . . . silently returned, your ears pressed against, or . . . or one eye into the crack so that the air smarts it sifting through. HAVE YOU COME BACK? HAVE YOU NOT LEFT ME? [*Pause.*] No. No one. Out in the night . . . nothing. Night? No; what then? IS IT NIGHT . . . OR DAY? [*Great weariness.*] Or does it matter? No. How long wilt thou forget me, O Lord? Forever? How long wilt thou hide thy face from me? How long shall my enemy . . . I . . . can . . . barely . . . feel. Which is a sign. A change, at any rate. [*To the rooftops again.*] I DO NOT UNDERSTAND, O LORD, MY GOD, WHAT THOU WILT HAVE OF ME! [*More conversational.*] I have never dreamed of it, never imagined what it would be like. I have – oh, yes – dwelt [*laughs at the word*] . . . dwelt . . . . on the *fact* of it, the . . . principle, but I have not imagined dying. Death . . . yes. Not being, but not the act of . . . dying? ALICE!? [*Laughs softly.*] Oh, Alice, why hast *thou* forsaken

me? [*Leans his head back to see the model.*] Hast thou? Alice?
Hast thou forsaken me ... with ... all the others?
[*Laughs again.*] Come bring me my slippers and my pipe,
and push the dog into the room. Bring me my slippers, the
sacramental wine, [*little boy*] my cookie? [*usual again*] ...
come bring me my ease, come sit with me ... and watch
me as I die. Alice? ALICE!? [*To himself.*] There is nothing; there is no one. [*Wheedling a little.*] Come talk to me;
come sit by my right hand ... *on* the one hand ... come
sit with me and hold my ... what? Then come and talk;
tell me how it goes, Alice. [*Laughs.*] 'Raise high the roof-
beam, for the bridegroom comes.' Oh, what a priesthood
is this! Oh, what a range of duties, and such parishioners,
and such a chapel for my praise. [*Turns some, leans toward
the model, where the chapel light shines.*] Oh, what a priesthood, see my chapel, how it ...

[*Suddenly the light in the chapel in the model goes out.*
JULIAN *starts, makes a sound of surprise and fear.*]

Alice? ... God? SOMEONE? Come to Julian as he ...
ebbs.

[*We begin to hear it now, faintly at first, slowly growing, so
faintly at first it is subliminal: the heartbeat ... thump
thump ... thump thump ... And the breathing ... the
intake taking one thump-thump, the exhaling the next.*
JULIAN *neither senses nor hears it yet, however.*]

Come, comfort him, warm him. He has not been a wilful
man ... Oh, wilful in his ... cry to serve, but gentle,
would not cause pain, but bear it, *would* bear it ... has,
even. Not much, I suppose. One man's share is not ...
another's burden. [*Notices the wig on the phrenological head;
crawls a bit toward it; half kneels in front of it.*] Thou art my
bride? Thou? For thee have I done my life? Grown to
love, entered in, bent ... accepted? For thee? Is that
the ... awful humour? Art thou the true arms, when the
warm flesh I touched ... rested against, was ... nothing?

And *she* . . . was not real? Is thy stare the true look? Un-blinking, outward, through, to some horizon? And her eyes . . . warm, accepting, were they . . . not real? Art thou my bride? [*To the ceiling again.*] Ah God! Is that the humour? THE ABSTRACT? . . . REAL? THE REST? . . . FALSE? [*To himself, with terrible irony.*] It is what I have wanted, have insisted on. Have nagged . . . for. [*Looking about the room, raging.*] IS THIS MY PRIESTHOOD, THEN? THIS WORLD? THEN COME AND SHOW THYSELF! BRIDE? GOD?

[*Silence; we hear the heartbeats and the breathing some.*]
SHOW THYSELF! I DEMAND THEE! [JULIAN *crawls back toward the model; faces it, back to the audience, addresses it.*] SHOW THYSELF! FOR THEE I HAVE GAMBLED . . . MY SOUL? I DEMAND THY PRESENCE. ALICE!

[*The sounds become louder now, as, in the model, the light fades in the bedroom, begins to move across an upper storey.*
JULIAN's *reaction is a muffled cry.*]
AGHH! [*On his hands and knees he backs off a little from the model, still staring at it.*] You . . . thou . . . art . . . coming to me? [*Frightened and angry.*] ABSTRACTION? . . . ABSTRACTION! . . . [*Sad, defeated.*] Art coming to me. [*A shivered prayer, quick.*] How long wilt thou forget me, O Lord? Forever? How long wilt thou hide thy face from me? . . . Consider and hear me, O Lord, my God. [*Shouted now.*] CONSIDER AND HEAR ME, O LORD, MY GOD. LIGHTEN MY EYES LEST I SLEEP THE SLEEP OF DEATH.

[*The lights keep moving; the sounds become louder.*]
BUT I HAVE TRUSTED IN THY MERCY, O LORD. HOW LONG WILT THOU FORGET ME? [*Softly, whining.*] How long wilt thou hide thy face from me? COME, BRIDE! COME, GOD! COME!

[*The breathing and heartbeats are much, much louder now. The lights descend a stairway in the model.* JULIAN *turns, backs against the model, his arms way to the side of him.*]

Alice? [*Fear and trembling.*] Alice? ALICE? MY GOD, WHY
HAST THOU FORSAKEN ME?

[*A great shadow, or darkening, fills the stage; it is the shadow
of a great presence filling the room. The area on* JULIAN *and
around him stays in some light, but, for the rest, it is as if ink
were moving through paper toward a focal point. The sounds
become enormous.* JULIAN *is aware of the presence in the
room, 'sees' it, in the sense that his eyes, his head move to
all areas of the room, noticing his engulfment. He almost-
whispers loudly.*]

The bridegroom waits for thee, my Alice . . . is thine. O
Lord, my God, I have awaited thee, have served thee in
thy . . . ALICE? [*His arms are wide, should resemble a
crucifixion. With his hands on the model, he will raise his body
some, backed full up against it.*] ALICE? . . . GOD?

[*The sounds are deafening.* JULIAN *smiles faintly.*]

I accept thee, Alice, for thou art come to me. God, Alice
. . . I accept thy will.

[*Sounds continue,* JULIAN *dies, head bows, body relaxes
some, arms stay wide in the crucifixion. Sounds continue
thusly: thrice after the death . . . thump* thump *thump*
thump *thump* thump. *Absolute silence for two beats. The
lights on* JULIAN *fade slowly to black. Only then, when all
is black, does the curtain slowly fall.*]

BOX *and*
QUOTATIONS FROM
CHAIRMAN MAO TSE-TUNG

First performed at the Studio Arena Theatre,
Buffalo, New York, 6 March 1968

Box

THE VOICE OF RUTH WHITE

Quotations from Chairman Mao Tse-Tung

CHAIRMAN MAO	*Conrad Yama*
LONG-WINDED LADY	*Lucille Patton*
OLD WOMAN	*Jenny Egan*
MINISTER	*William Needles*

Directed by ALAN SCHNEIDER

First performed in New York City
at the Billy Rose Theatre, 30 September 1968

Box

THE VOICE OF RUTH WHITE

Quotations from Chairman Mao Tse-Tung

CHAIRMAN MAO	*Wyman Pendleton*
LONG-WINDED LADY	*Nancy Kelly*
OLD WOMAN	*Sudie Bond*
MINISTER	*George Bartenieff*

Directed by ALAN SCHNEIDER

INTRODUCTION

While it is true that these two short plays – *Box* and *Quotations from Chairman Mao Tse-tung* – are separate works, were conceived at different though not distant moments, stand by themselves, and can be played one without the company of the other, I feel that they are more effective performed enmeshed.

Even more ... *Quotations from Chairman Mao Tse-tung* would most probably not have been written had not *Box* been composed beforehand, and *Mao* is, therefore, an outgrowth of and extension of the shorter play. As well, I have attempted, in these two related plays, several experiments having to do – in the main – with the application of musical form to dramatic structure, and the use of *Box* as a parenthesis around *Mao* is part of that experiment.

I may as well insist right now that these two plays are quite simple. By that I mean that while technically they are fairly complex and they do demand from an audience quite close attention, their content can be apprehended without much difficulty. All that one need do is – quite simply – relax and let the plays happen. That, and be willing to approach the dramatic experience without a preconception of what the nature of the dramatic experience should be.

I recall that when a play of mine called *Tiny Alice* opened in New York City a few years ago the majority of the critics wrote in their reviews – such as they were – that the play was far too complicated and obscure for the audience to understand. Leaving to one side the thoughts one might have about the assumption on the part of the critics that what they found confusing would necessarily confound an audience, this reportage had a most curious effect on the audiences that viewed the play. At the preview performances of *Tiny Alice* the audiences – while hardly to a man sympathetic to the play – found it quite clear; while later – after the critics had spoken on it – the audiences were very confused. The play had not changed one whit; a label had merely been attached to it, and what was experienced was the label and not the nature of the goods.

A playwright – unless he is creating escapist romances (an honourable occupation, of course) – has two obligations: first, to make some statement about the condition of 'man' (as it is put) and, second, to make some statement about the nature of the art form with which he is working. In both instances he must attempt change. In the first instance – since very few serious plays are written to glorify the status quo – the playwright must try to alter his society; in the second instance – since art must move, or wither – the playwright must try to alter the forms within which his precursors have had to work. And I believe that an audience has an obligation to be interested in and sympathetic to these aims – certainly to the second of them. Therefore, an audience has an obligation (to itself, to the art form in which it is participating, and even to the playwright) to be willing to experience a work on its own terms.

I said before that these two plays are simple (as well as complex), and they *are* simple once they are experienced relaxed and without a weighing of their methods against more familiar ones.

EDWARD ALBEE

BOX

Curtain rises in darkness. Lights go up slowly to reveal the outline of a large cube. The cube should take up almost all of a small stage opening. The side facing the audience is open, but we should see the other five sides clearly, therefore the interior of the cube should be distorted, smaller at the backstage side, for example; also, none of the sides should be exactly square in shape, but the angles of distortion should not be very great – not so great as to call attention to themselves and destroy the feeling of a cube. When the lights are fully up on the cube – quite bright light which stays constant until the final dim-out – there should be five seconds' silence.

VOICE:

> [*The* VOICE *should not come from the stage, but should seem to be coming from near by the spectator – from the back or the sides of the theatre. The* VOICE *of a woman; not young, but not ancient, either: fiftyish. Neither a sharp, crone's voice, but not refined. A Middle Western farm woman's voice would be best.*
>
> *Matter-of-fact; announcement of a subject.*]

Box.

> [*Five-second silence.*]

Box.

> [*Three-second silence.*]

Nicely done. Well put . . .

> [*Pause.*]

. . . together. Box.

> [*Three-second silence. More conversational now.*]

Room inside for a sedia d'ondalo, which, in English – for that is Italian – would be, is, rocking chair. Room to rock. *And* room to move about in . . . some. Enough.

> [*Three-second silence.*]

Carpentry is among the arts going out . . . or crafts, if you're of a nonclassical disposition. There are others:

other arts which have gone down to craft and which are going further . . . walls, brick walls, music . . .

[*Pause.*]

. . . the making of good bread if you won't laugh; living. Many arts: all craft now . . . and going further. But *this* is solid, perfect joins . . . good work. Knock and there's no give – no give of sound, I mean. A thud; no hollow. Oh, very good work; fine timber, and so fastidious, like when they shined the bottoms of the shoes . . . *and* the instep. Not only where you might *expect* they'd shine the bottoms if they *did* . . . but even the instep.

[*Two-second silence. Grudging, but not very.*]

And other crafts have come up . . . if not to replace, then . . . occupy.

[*Tiny laugh.*]

Nature abhors, among so many, so much else . . . amongst so much, us, itself, they say, vacuum.

[*Five-second silence. A listing.*]

System as conclusion, in the sense of method as an end, the dice so big you can hardly throw them any more.

[*Some awe, some sadness.*]

Seven hundred million babies dead in the time it takes, took, to knead the dough to make a proper loaf. Well, little wonder so many . . . went . . . cut off, said no instead of hanging on.

[*Three-second silence.*]

Apathy, I think.

[*Five-second silence.*]

Inevitability. And progress is merely a direction, movement.

[*Earnest.*]

When it was *simple* . . .

[*Light, self-mocking laugh.*]

Ah, well, yes, when it was simple.

[*Three-second silence. Wistful.*]

BOX   129

Beautiful, beautiful box.

[*Three-second silence.*]

And room enough to walk around in, take a turn.

[*Tiny pause.*]

If only they had *told* us! Clearly! When it was clear that
we were not only corrupt – for there is nothing that is
not, or little – but corrupt to the selfishness, to the corruption that we should die to keep it . . . go under rather
than . . .

[*Three-second silence. Sigh.*]

Oh, my.

[*Five-second silence.*]

Or was it the milk? *That* may have been the moment:
spilling and spilling and killing all those children to make
a point. A penny or two, and a symbol at that, and I
suppose the children were symbolic, too, though they
died, and couldn't stop. Once it starts – gets to a certain
point – the momentum is too much. But spilling milk!

[*Two-second silence. Firmly felt.*]

Oh, shame! [*A little schoolmarmish.*] The *Pope* warned us;
he said so. There are no possessions, he said; so long as
there are some with nothing we have no right to anything.

[*Two-second silence.*]

It's the *little* things, the *small* cracks. Oh, for every
pound of milk they spill you can send a check to someone,
but that does not unspill. That it *can* be *done* is the crack.
And if you go back to a partita . . . ahhhhh, what when
it makes you cry!? Not from the beauty of it, but from
solely that you cry from loss . . . so precious. When art
begins to hurt . . . when art begins to hurt, it's time to
look around. Yes it is.

[*Three-second silence.*]

Yes it is.

[*Three-second silence.*]

No longer just great beauty which takes you more to everything, but a reminder! And not of what *can* . . . but what *has*. Yes, when art hurts . . .

[*Three-second silence.*]

Box.

[*Two-second silence.*]

And room enough to move around, except like a fly. That would be *very* good! [*Rue.*] Yes, but so would so much.

[*Two-second silence. Schoolmarmish.*]

Here is the thing about tension and the tonic – the important thing.

[*Pause.*]

The release of tension is the return to consonance; no matter how far travelled, one comes back, not circular, not to the starting point, but a . . . setting down again, and the beauty of art is order – not what is familiar, necessarily, but order . . . on its own terms.

[*Two-second silence. Sigh.*]

So much . . . flies. A billion birds at once, black net skimming the ocean, or the Monarchs that time, that island, blown by the wind, but going straight . . . in a direction. Order!

[*Two-second silence.*]

And six sides to bounce it all off of.

[*Three-second silence. Brave start again.*]

When the beauty of it reminds us of *loss*. Instead of the attainable. When it tells us what we cannot have . . . well, then . . . it no longer relates . . . *does* it. That is the thing about music. That is why we cannot listen any more.

[*Pause.*]

Because we cry.

[*Three-second silence.*]

And *if* he says, or *she* . . . why are you doing that?, and, and your only honest response is: art hurts . . .

[*Little laugh.*]

BOX 131

Well.

[*Five-second silence.*]

Look! More birds! Another . . . sky of them.

[*Five-second silence.*]

It is not a matter of garden, or straight lines, or even . . .
morality. It's only when you can't come back; when you
get in some distant key; that when you say, the tonic! the
tonic! and they say, what is *that*? It's *then*.

[*Three-second silence.*]

There! More! A thousand, and one below them, moving
fast in the opposite way!

[*Two-second silence.*]

What was it used to frighten me? Bell buoys and sea
gulls; the *sound* of them, at night, in a fog, when I was
very young.

[*A little laugh.*]

Before I had ever seen them, before I had heard them.
[*Some wonder.*] But I knew what they *were* . . . a thousand
miles from the sea. Land-locked, never been, and yet the
sea sounds . . .

[*Three-second silence. Very matter-of-fact.*]

Well, we can exist with *any*thing; with*out*. There's little
that we need to have to go on . . . evolving. Goodness;
we all died when we were thirty once. Now, much
younger. Much.

[*Suddenly aware of something.*] But it *couldn't* have been fog,
not the sea-fog. Not way back *there*. It was the memory
of it, to be seen and proved later. And more! and more!
they're all moving! The memory of what we have not
known. And so it is with the fog, which I had never seen,
yet knew it. And the resolution of a chord; no difference.

[*Three-second silence.*]

And even that can happen here, I guess. But unprovable.
Ahhhhh. That makes the difference, does it *not*. Nothing

can seep here except the memory of what I'll not prove.

[*Two-second silence. Sigh.*]

Well, we give up something for something.

[*Three-second silence. Listing again; pleased.*]

Sturdy, light . . . interesting . . . in its way. Room enough for a sedia d'ondalo, which is the Italian of . . . or for . . . *of*, I prefer . . . The Italian of rocking chair.

[*Three-second silence.*]

When art hurts. That is what to remember.

[*Two-second silence.*]

What to look for. Then the corruption . . .

[*Three-second silence.*]

Then the corruption is complete.

[*Five-second silence. The sound of bell buoys and sea gulls begins, faintly, growing, but never very loud.*]

Nothing belongs.

[*Three-second silence. Great sadness.*]

Look; more of them; a black net . . . skimming.

[*Pause.*]

And just one . . . moving beneath . . . in the opposite way.

[*Three-second silence. Very sad, supplicating.*]

Milk.

[*Three-second silence.*]

Milk.

[*Five-second silence. Wistful.*]

Box.

[*Silence, except for the sound of bell buoys and sea gulls. Very slow fading of lights to black, sound of bell buoys and sea gulls fading with the light.*]

QUOTATIONS
FROM CHAIRMAN
MAO TSE-TUNG

The outline of the cube remains; the set for QUOTATIONS FROM CHAIRMAN MAO TSE-TUNG appears within the outlines of the cube during the brief blackout.

CHARACTERS

CHAIRMAN MAO

Should be played, ideally, by an Oriental actor who resembles Mao. However, the role can be played either with makeup or a face mask. In any event, an attempt should be made to make the actor resemble Mao as much as possible. MAO *speaks rather like a teacher. He does not raise his voice; he is not given to histrionics. His tone is always reasonable, sometimes a little sad; occasionally a half-smile will appear. He may wander about the set a little, but, for the most part, he should keep his place by the railing.* MAO *always speaks to the audience. He is aware of the other characters, but he must never look at them or suggest in any way that anything they say is affecting his words. When I say that* MAO *always addresses the audience I do not mean that he must look them in the eye constantly. Once he has made it clear that he is addressing them he may keep that intention clear in any way he likes – looking away, speaking to only one person, whatever.*

LONG-WINDED LADY

A lady of sixty. I care very little about how she looks so long as she looks very average and upper middle-class. Nothing exotic; nothing strange. She should, I think, stay pretty much to her deck chair. She never speaks to the audience. Sometimes she is clearly speaking to the MINISTER; *more often she is speaking both for his benefit and her own. She can withdraw entirely into self from time to time. She uses the* MINISTER *as a sounding board.*

OLD WOMAN

Shabby, poor, without being so in a comedy sense. She has a bag with her. An orange; an apple, one or two cans: beans, canned meat. She will eat from these occasionally. Her bag also contains a fork, or a spoon, a napkin, and a can-opener. She is aware of everybody, but speaks only to the audience. Her reading of her poem can have some emotion to it, though never too much. It should be made clear, though, that while the subject of her speeches is dear to her heart, a close matter, she is reciting a poem. She may look at the other characters from time to time, but what she says must never seem to come from what any of the others has said. She might nod in agreement with MAO *now and again, or shake her head over the plight of the* LONG-WINDED LADY. *She should stay in one place, up on something.*

MINISTER

Has no lines, and stays in his deck chair. He must try to pay close attention to the LONG-WINDED LADY, *though – nod, shake his head, cluck, put an arm tentatively out, etc. He must also keep busy with his pipe and pouch and matches. He should doze off from time to time. He must never make the audience feel he is looking at them or is aware of them. Also, he is not aware of either* MAO *or the* OLD WOMAN. *He is seventy or so, has white or grey hair, a clerical collar. A florid face would be nice. If a thin actor is playing the role, however, then make the face sort of grey-yellow-white.*

GENERAL COMMENTS

For this play to work according to my intention, careful attention must be paid to what I have written about the characters: to whom they speak; to whom they may and may not react; how they speak; how they move or do not. Alteration from the patterns I have set may be interesting, but I fear they will destroy the attempt of the experiment: musical structure – form and counterpoint. Primarily the characters must seem interested in what they themselves are doing and saying. While the lines must not be read metronome-exact, I feel that a certain set rhythm will come about, quite of itself. No one rushes in on the end of anyone else's speech; no one waits too long. I have indicated, quite precisely, within the speeches of the LONG-WINDED LADY, by means of commas, periods, semi-colons, dashes and dots (as well as parenthetical stage directions), the speech rhythms. Please observe them carefully, for they were not thrown in, like herbs on a salad, to be mixed about. I have italicized words I want stressed. I have capitalized for loudness, and used exclamation points for emphasis. There are one or two seeming questions that I have left the question mark off of. This was done on purpose, as an out-loud reading will make self-evident.

The deck of an ocean liner. Bright daylight, that particular kind of brightness that is possible only in mid-ocean.

CHAIRMAN MAO: There is an ancient Chinese fable called 'The foolish old man who removed the mountains.' It tells of an old man who lived in Northern China long, long ago, and was known as the foolish old man of the north mountains. His house faced south and beyond his doorway stood the two great peaks, Taihand and Wang-wu, obstructing the way. With great determination, he led his sons in digging up these mountains, hoe in hand. Another greybeard, known as the wise old man, saw them and said derisively, 'How silly of you to do this! It is quite impossible for you few to dig up those two huge mountains.' The foolish old man replied, 'When I die, my sons will carry on; when they die there will be my grandsons, and then their sons and grandsons, and so on to infinity. High as they are, the mountains cannot grow any higher and with every bit we dig, they will be that much lower. Why can't we clear them away?' Having refuted the wise old man's wrong view, he went on digging every day, unshaken in his conviction. God was moved by this, and he sent down two angels, who carried the mountains away on their backs. Today, two big mountains lie like a dead weight on the Chinese people. One is imperialism, the other is feudalism. The Chinese Communist Party has long made up its mind to dig them up. We must persevere and work unceasingly, and we, too, will touch God's heart. Our God is none other than the masses of the Chinese people. If they stand up and dig together with us, why can't these two mountains be cleared away?

LONG-WINDED LADY: Well, I daresay it's hard to comprehend . . . I mean: *I* . . . at this remove . . . *I* find it hard to, well, not comprehend, but believe, or accept, if you will. So long ago! So much since. But there it was: Splash!

OLD WOMAN: 'Over the Hill to the Poor-House.'

LONG-WINDED LADY: Well, not splash, exactly, more sound than that, more of a . . . [*little laugh*] no, I can't do that – imitate it: for I only *imagine* . . . what it must have sounded like to . . . an onlooker. An overseer. Not to *me*; Lord knows! Being *in* it. Or doing it, rather.

CHAIRMAN MAO: In drawing up plans, handling affairs or thinking over problems, we must proceed from the fact that China has six hundred million people, and we must never forget this fact.

OLD WOMAN: By Will Carleton.

LONG-WINDED LADY: No. To an onlooker it would not have been splash, but a sort of . . . different sound, and I try to imagine what it would have been like – *sounded* like – had *I* not been . . . well, so involved, if you know what I mean. And *I* was so *busy* . . . I didn't pay attention, or, if I did . . . that part of it doesn't re . . . recall itself. Retain is the, is what I started.

OLD WOMAN: 'Over the Hill to the Poor-House' – a poem by Will Carleton.

CHAIRMAN MAO: Apart from their other characteristics, the outstanding thing about China's six hundred million people is that they are 'poor and blank'. This may seem a bad thing, but in reality it is a good thing. Poverty gives rise to the desire for change, the desire for action and the desire for revolution. On a blank sheet of paper free from any mark, the freshest and most beautiful characters can be written, the freshest and most beautiful pictures can be painted.

LONG-WINDED LADY: And so high!

OLD WOMAN: Over the hill to the poor-house – I can't quite make it clear!

Over the hill to the poor-house – it seems so horrid queer!
Many a step I've taken, a-toilin' to and fro,
But this is a sort of journey I never thought to go.

LONG-WINDED LADY: I'd never imagined it – naturally! It's not what one *would*. The *echo* of a sound, or the remembering of a sound having happened. No; that's not right either. For *them*; for the theoretical . . . on-watcher.

[*Pause.*]

Plut! Yes!

CHAIRMAN MAO: Communism is at once a complete system of proletarian ideology and a new social system. It is different from any other ideological and social system, and is the most complete, progressive, revolutionary and rational system in human history. The communist ideological and social system alone is full of youth and vitality, sweeping the world with the momentum of an avalanche and the force of a thunderbolt.

LONG-WINDED LADY: Exactly: plut!

OLD WOMAN: Over the hill to the poor-house I'm trudgin' my weary way –

I, a woman of seventy, and only a trifle grey –
I, who am smart an' chipper, for all the years I've told,
As many another woman that's only half as old.

LONG-WINDED LADY: And then, with the wind, and the roar of the engines and the sea . . . maybe not even that, not even . . . plut! But, some slight sound, or . . . or the creation of one! The invention! What is that about consequence? Oh, *you* know! Everything has its consequence? Or, every action a reaction; something. But maybe nothing at all, no real sound, but the invention of one. I mean, if you see it happening . . . the, the thing . . . landing, and the spray, the sea parting, as it were . . .

well, then . . . one makes a sound . . . in one's mind . . . to, to correspond to the sound one . . . didn't . . . hear. Yes?

CHAIRMAN MAO: Imperialism will not last long because it always does evil things.

OLD WOMAN: 'Over the Hill to the Poor-House.'

CHAIRMAN MAO: It persists in grooming and supporting reactionaries in all countries who are against the people; it has forcibly seized many colonies and semi-colonies and many military bases, and it threatens the peace with atomic war.

OLD WOMAN: By Will Carleton.

CHAIRMAN MAO: Thus, forced by imperialism to do so, more than ninety per cent of the people of the world are rising or will rise up in struggle against it.

OLD WOMAN: Over the hill to the poor-house I'm trudgin' my weary way –

I, a woman of seventy, and only a trifle grey.

CHAIRMAN MAO: Yet imperialism is still alive, still running amuck in Asia, Africa and Latin America. In the West, imperialism is still oppressing the people at home. This situation must change.

OLD WOMAN: I, who am smart an' chipper, for all the years I've told,

As many another woman that's only half as old.

CHAIRMAN MAO: It is the task of the people of the whole world to put an end to the aggression and oppression perpetrated by imperialism, and chiefly by U.S. imperialism.

LONG-WINDED LADY: Yes. I think so.

CHAIRMAN MAO: Historically, all reactionary forces on the verge of extinction invariably conduct a last desperate struggle against the revolutionary forces, and some revolutionaries are apt to be deluded for a time by this phenomenon of outward strength but inner weakness, failing to grasp the essential fact that the enemy is nearing extinction while they themselves are approaching victory.

LONG-WINDED LADY: I remember once when I broke my finger, or my thumb, and I was very little, and they said, you've broken your thumb, look, you've broken your thumb, and there wasn't any pain . . . not *yet*; not for that first moment, just . . . just an absence of sensation – an interesting lack of anything.

OLD WOMAN: 'Over the Hill to the Poor-House.'

LONG-WINDED LADY: When they said it again, look, you've broken your thumb, not only did I scream, as if some knife had ripped my leg down, from hip to ankle, all through the sinews, laying bare the bone . . . not only did I scream as only children can – adults do it differently: there's an animal protest there, a revenge, something . . . something other – not only did I scream, but I manufactured the pain. Right then! Before the hurt could have come through, I made it happen.

　[*Pause.*]

Well; we do that.

OLD WOMAN: What is the use of heapin' on me a pauper's shame?

Am I lazy or crazy? am I blind or lame?

True, I am not so supple, nor yet so awful stout;

But charity ain't no favour, if one can live without.

LONG-WINDED LADY: Yes; we do that: we make it happen a little before it need.

　[*Pause.*]

And so it might have been with someone watching – and maybe even to those who *were*. Who *were* watching. And there were, or I'd not be here.

　[*Pause.*]

I daresay.

　[*Pause.*]

The sound manufactured. Lord knows, if *I* had been among the . . . non-participators I should have done it, too; no doubt. Plup! Plut! Whichever. I'm sure *I* should have . . . if I'd seen it all the *way*, now. I mean, if I'd caught just the final instant, without time to relate the event to its environment – the thing happening to the thing happened *to* . . . then I doubt I would have. Nor would anyone . . . or most.

CHAIRMAN MAO: The imperialists and their running dogs, the Chinese reactionaries, will not resign themselves to defeat in this land of China.

OLD WOMAN: What is the use of heapin' on me a pauper's shame?

Am I lazy or crazy? Am I blind or lame?

CHAIRMAN MAO: All this we must take fully into account.

LONG-WINDED LADY: But just imagine what it must have been like . . . to be one of the . . . watchers! How . . . well, is marvellous the proper word, I wonder? Yes, I suspect. I mean, how often? ! It's not too common an occurrence, to have it . . . plummet by! One is standing there, admiring, or faintly sick, or just plain throwing up, but how often is one *there*. *Ever*! Well, inveterates; yes; but for the casual crosser . . . not too often, and one would have to be exactly in place, at exactly the proper time, and alert! Very alert in . . . by nature, and able to relate what one sees to what is happening. Oh, I remember the time the taxi went berserk and killed those people!

CHAIRMAN MAO: Riding roughshod everywhere, U.S. imperialism has made itself the enemy of the people of the world and has increasingly isolated itself. Those who refuse to be enslaved will never be cowed by the atom bombs and hydrogen bombs in the hands of the U.S. imperialists. The raging tide of the people of the world against the U.S. aggressors is irresistible. Their struggle against U.S. imperialism and its lackeys will assuredly win still greater victories.

LONG-WINDED LADY: Well, it didn't go berserk, of course, for it *is* a machine: a taxi. Nor did the driver . . .

go berserk. Out of control, though! The driver lost and out of control it went! *Up* on the sidewalk, bowling them down like whatchamacallems, then crash!, into the store front, the splash of glass and then on fire. How many dead? Ten? Twelve? And I had just come out with the crullers.

OLD WOMAN: I am ready and willin' an' anxious any day
To work for a decent livin', an' pay my honest way;
For I can earn my victuals, an' more too, I'll be bound,
If anybody is willin' to only have me 'round.

LONG-WINDED LADY: The bag of crullers, and a smile on my face for everyone liked them so, and there it was! Careen . . . and dying . . . and all that glass. And I remember thinking: it's a movie! They're shooting some scenes right here on the street.

[*Pause.*]

They weren't, of course. It was real death, and real glass, and the fire, and the . . . people crying, and the crowds, and the smoke. Oh, it was real enough, but it took me time to know it. The mind does that.

CHAIRMAN MAO: If the U.S. monopoly capitalist groups persist in pushing their policies of aggression and war, the day is bound to come when they will be hanged by the people of the whole world. The same fate awaits the accomplices of the United States.

OLD WOMAN: I am ready and willin' an' anxious any day
To work for a decent livin', an' pay my honest way;
For I can earn my victuals, an' more too, I'll be bound,
If anybody is willin' to only have me 'round.

LONG-WINDED LADY: They're making a movie! What a nice conclusion, coming out with the crullers, still hot, with a separate little bag for the powdered sugar, of course it's a movie! One doesn't come out like that to carnage! Dead people and the wounded; glass all over and . . . confusion. One . . . concludes things – and if those things and what is really there don't . . . are not the *same* . . . well! . . . it would usually be better if it were so. The mind does that: it helps.

CHAIRMAN MAO: To achieve a lasting world peace, we must further develop our friendship and cooperation with the fraternal countries in the socialist camp and strengthen our solidarity with all peace-loving countries.

LONG-WINDED LADY: The mind does that.

CHAIRMAN MAO: We must endeavour to establish normal diplomatic relations, on the basis of mutual respect for territorial integrity and sovereignty and of equality and mutual benefit, with all countries willing to live together with us in peace.

LONG-WINDED LADY: It helps.

CHAIRMAN MAO: We must give active support to the national independence and liberation movement in Asia, Africa, and Latin America as well as to the peace movement and to just struggles in all the countries of the world.

VOICE, FROM BOX; Box.

LONG-WINDED LADY: So; if one happened to be there, by the rail, and not too discomfited, not in the sense of utterly defeated – though that would be more than enough – but in the sense of confused, or preoccupied, if one were not too preoccupied, and plummet! it went by! one, the mind, might be able to take it in, say: ah! there! there she goes! – or he; and manufacture the appropriate sound. But only then. And how many are expecting it!? Well, *I* am. *Now*. There isn't a rail I stand by, especially in full sun – my conditioning – that I'm not . . . already shuddering . . . *and* ready to manufacture the sound. [*Little laugh.*] Though not the sound *I* knew, for I was hardly thinking – a bit busy – but the sound I imagine someone else would have manufactured had *he* been there when I . . . woooosssh!! plut!! [*Little laugh.*]

VOICE, FROM BOX: Box.

OLD WOMAN: Once I was young an' han'some – I was, upon my soul –

Once my cheeks was roses, my eyes as black as coal;
And I can't remember, in them days, of hearin' people say,
For any kind of a reason, that I was in their way!

LONG-WINDED LADY: You never know until it's happened to you.

VOICE, FROM BOX: Many arts: all craft now ... and going further.

CHAIRMAN MAO: Our country and all the other socialist countries want peace; so do the peoples of all the countries of the world. The only ones who crave war and do not want peace are certain monopoly capitalist groups in a handful of imperialist countries which depend on aggression for their profits.

LONG-WINDED LADY: *Do* you.

VOICE, FROM BOX: Box.

CHAIRMAN MAO: Who are our enemies? Who are our friends?

LONG-WINDED LADY: *Do* you.

CHAIRMAN MAO: Our enemies are all those in league with imperialism; our closest friends are the entire semi-proletariat and petty bourgeoisie. As for the vacillating middle bourgeoisie, their right wing may become our enemy and their left wing may become our friend.

LONG-WINDED LADY: Falling! My goodness. What was it when one was little? That when you fell when you were dreaming you always woke up before you landed, or else you wouldn't and you'd be dead. That was it, I think. And I never wondered why, I merely took it for ... well, I *accepted* it. And, of course, I kept trying to dream of falling after I'd heard it ... tried so hard! ... and *couldn't*, naturally. Well, if we control the unconscious, we're either mad, or ... dull-witted.

OLD WOMAN: Once I was young an' han'some – I was, upon my soul.

LONG-WINDED LADY: I think I dreamt of falling again, though, but after I'd stopped trying to, but I don't think I landed. Not like what I've been telling you, though that was more seaing than landing, you might say . . . if you like a pun. Once, though! Once, I dreamt of falling straight up . . . or out, all in reverse, like the projector running backwards, what they used to do, for fun, in the shorts. [*Some wonder.*] Falling . . . *up*!

CHAIRMAN MAO: In the final analysis, national struggle is a matter of class struggle. Among the whites in the United States it is only the reactionary ruling circles who oppress the black people.

LONG-WINDED LADY: Falling . . . *up*!

CHAIRMAN MAO: They can in no way represent the workers, farmers, revolutionary intellectuals and other enlightened persons who comprise the overwhelming majority of the white people.

VOICE, FROM BOX: Seven hundred million babies dead in half the time it takes, took, to knead the dough to make a proper loaf. Well, little wonder so many . . .

LONG-WINDED LADY: Not rising, you understand: a definite . . . falling, but . . . up!

OLD WOMAN: 'Tain't no use of boastin', or talkin' over free,
But many a house an' home was open then to me;
Many a han'some offer I had from likely men,
And nobody ever hinted that I was a burden then!

LONG-WINDED LADY: Did I call them crullers? Well, I should *not* have; for they were not even doughnuts, but the centres . . . hearts is what they called them: the centre dough pinched out, or cut with a cutter and done like the rest, but solid, the size of a bantam egg, but round. Oh, they were good, and crisp, and all like air inside; hot, and you'd dip them in the confectioner's sugar. One could be quite a pig; everyone was; they were so good! You find them here and about still. Some, but not often.

OLD WOMAN: 'Over the Hill to the Poor-House.'

CHAIRMAN MAO: All reactionaries are paper tigers. In appearance, the reactionaries are terrifying, but in reality they are not so powerful. From a long-term point of view, it is not the reactionaries but the people who are really powerful.

VOICE, FROM BOX: Apathy, I think.

LONG-WINDED LADY: My husband used to say, don't leave her next to anything precipitous; there's bound to be a do; something will drop, or fall, her purse, her*self*. And, so, he had people be careful of me. Not that I'm fond of heights. I'm not unfriendly toward them – all that falling – but I have no . . . great affection.

[*Little pause.*]

Depths even less.

OLD WOMAN: By Will Carleton.

CHAIRMAN MAO: I have said that all the reputedly powerful reactionaries are merely paper tigers. The reason is that they are divorced from the people. Look! Was not Hitler a paper tiger? Was Hitler not over-thrown? I also said that the tsar of Russia, the emperor of China and Japanese imperialism were all paper tigers. As we know, they were all overthrown.

LONG-WINDED LADY: All that falling.

CHAIRMAN MAO: U.S. imperialism has not yet been over-thrown and it has the atom bomb. I believe it also will be overthrown. It, too, is a paper tiger.

LONG-WINDED LADY: And it became something of a joke, I suppose . . . I suppose. Where is she? Watch her! Don't let her near the edge! She'll occasion a do!

OLD WOMAN: And when to John I was married, sure he was good and smart,
But he and all the neighbours would own I done my part;

For life was all before me, an' I was young an' strong,
And I worked my best an' smartest in tryin' to get along.

LONG-WINDED LADY: He was a small man – my husband,
almost a miniature . . . not that I'm much of a giraffe.
Small . . . and precise . . . and contained . . . quiet
strength. The large emotions . . . *yes*, without them, what?
– all there, and full size, full scope, but when they came,
not a . . . spattering, but a single shaft, a careful aim. No
waste, as intense as anyone, but precise. Some people said
he was cold; or cruel. But he was merely accurate. Big
people ooze, and scatter, and knock over things nearby.
They give the impression – the illusion – of openness, of
spaces through which things pass – excuses, bypassings.
But small, and precise, and accurate don't . . . doesn't allow
for that . . . for that *impression*. He wasn't cruel at all.

CHAIRMAN MAO: The socialist system will eventually
replace the capitalist system; this is an objective law
independent of man's will. However much the reactionaries try to hold back the wheel of history, sooner or later
revolution will take place and will inevitably triumph.

OLD WOMAN: Over the hill to the poor-house – I can't
quite make it clear.

LONG-WINDED LADY: *Or* cold. Neat; accurate; precise.
In everything. All our marriage. Except dying. Except
that . . . dreadful death.

CHAIRMAN MAO: The imperialists and domestic reactionaries will certainly not take their defeat lying down and
they will struggle to the last ditch. This is inevitable and
beyond all doubt, and under no circumstances must we
relax our vigilance.

LONG-WINDED LADY: That dreadful death – all that he
was not: large, random, inaccurate – in the sense of off-
shoots from the major objective. A spattering cancer!
Spread enough and you're bound to kill *some*thing. Don't
aim! Engulf! Imprecision!

VOICE, FROM BOX: When it was *simple* . . . [*Light, self-mocking laugh.*] Ah, well, yes, when it was simple.

OLD WOMAN: And so we worked together: and life was hard, but gay,

With now and then a baby to cheer us on our way;

Till we had half a dozen: an' all growed clean an' neat,

An' went to school like others, an' had enough to eat.

LONG-WINDED LADY: Don't let her near the edge!

CHAIRMAN MAO: Make trouble, fail, make trouble again, fail again . . . till their doom; that is the logic of the imperialists and all reactionaries the world over in dealing with the people's cause, and they will never go against this logic. This is a Marxist law.

LONG-WINDED LADY: Don't let her near the edge.

CHAIRMAN MAO: When we say 'imperialism is ferocious', we mean that its nature will never change, that the imperialists will never lay down their butcher knives, that they will never become Buddhas, till their doom. Fight, fail, fight again, fail again, fight again . . . till their victory; that is the logic of the people, and they too will never go against this logic. This is another Marxist law.

LONG-WINDED LADY: But I hadn't thought I *was*. Well, yes, of course I *was* . . . but guarded . . . well guarded. Or, so I *thought*. It doesn't happen terribly often – falling . . . by indirection.

[*Pause.*]

Does it?

OLD WOMAN: An' so we worked for the child'rn, and raised 'em every one;

Worked for 'em summer and winter, just as we ought to've done;

Only perhaps we humoured 'em, which some good folks condemn,

But every couple's child'rn's a heap the best to them!

VOICE, FROM BOX: Oh, shame!

LONG-WINDED LADY: Not death: I didn't mean death. I meant ... falling off. *That* isn't done too often by indirection. *Is* it! Death! Well, my God, of course; yes. Almost always, 'less you take the notion of the collective ... thing, which *must allow* for it, take it into account: I mean, if all the rest is part of a ... predetermination, or something that has already happened – in principle – well, under *those* conditions *any* chaos becomes order. Any chaos at all.

VOICE, FROM BOX: Oh, shame!

CHAIRMAN MAO: Everything reactionary is the same; if you don't hit it, it won't fall.

VOICE, FROM BOX: Oh, shame!

CHAIRMAN MAO: This is also like sweeping the floor; as a rule, where the broom does not reach, the dust will not vanish of itself. Nor will the enemy perish of himself. The aggressive forces of U.S. imperialism will not step down from the stage of history of their own accord.

VOICE, FROM BOX: The *Pope* warned us; *he* said so. There are no possessions, he said; so long as there are some with nothing we have no right to anything.

LONG-WINDED LADY: And the thing about boats is ... you're burned ... always ... sun ... haze ... mist ... deep night ... all the spectrum down. Something. Burning.

CHAIRMAN MAO: Everything reactionary is the same; if you don't hit it, it won't fall.

LONG-WINDED LADY: I sat up one night – oh, *before* it happened, though it doesn't matter – I mean, on a deck chair, like this, well away from the ... possibility, but I sat up, and the moon was small, as it always is, on the northern route, well out, and I *bathed* in the night, and perhaps my daughter came up from dancing, though I don't think so ... dancing down there with a man, well, young enough to be her husband.

OLD WOMAN: For life was all before me, an' I was young
an' strong,
And I worked the best that I could in tryin' to get
along.

LONG-WINDED LADY: Though not. Not her husband.

CHAIRMAN MAO: Classes struggle; some classes triumph,
others are eliminated. Such is history, such is the history
of civilization for thousands of years. To interpret history
from this viewpoint is historical materialism; standing in
opposition to this viewpoint is historical idealism.

LONG-WINDED LADY: Though not. Not her husband.

CHAIRMAN MAO: No political party can possibly lead a
great revolutionary movement to victory unless it possesses revolutionary theory and a knowledge of history
and has a profound grasp of the practical movement.

LONG-WINDED LADY: And what I mean is: the burn;
sitting in the dim moon, with not the sound of the
orchestra, but the *possible* sound of it – therefore, I
suppose, the same – the daughter, *my* daughter, and me
up here, up *there* – this one? No. – and being burned! In
that – what I said – that all seasons, all lights, all . . .
well, one never returns from a voyage the same.

VOICE, FROM BOX: It's the *little* things, the *small* cracks.

OLD WOMAN: Strange how much we think of our blessed
little ones! –
I'd have died for my daughters, I'd have died for my
sons;
And God he made that rule of love; but when we're old
and grey,
I've noticed it sometimes somehow fails to work the other
way.

LONG-WINDED LADY: His scrotum was large, and not
only for a small man, I think, as I remember back – and
am I surmising my comparisons here, or telling you something loose about my past? [*Shrugs*.]

CHAIRMAN MAO: Classes struggle; some classes triumph, others are eliminated.

LONG-WINDED LADY: What does it matter now, this late? – large, and not of the loose type, but thick, and leather, marvellously creased and like a neat, full sack. And his penis, too; of a neat proportion; ample, but not of that size which moves us so in retrospect ... or is supposed to. Circumcised ... well, no, not really, but trained back, *to* it; trained; like everything; nothing surprising, but always there, and ample. Do I shock you?

VOICE, FROM BOX: And if you go back to a partita ...

CHAIRMAN MAO: Such is history.

LONG-WINDED LADY: Do I *shock* you?

CHAIRMAN MAO: The commanders and fighters of the entire Chinese people's Liberation Army absolutely must not relax in the least their will to fight; any thinking that relaxes the will to fight and belittles the enemy is wrong.

LONG-WINDED LADY: That is the last I have in mind. My intention is only to remember.

OLD WOMAN: Strange how much we think of our blessed little ones!

CHAIRMAN MAO: I hold that it is bad as far as we are concerned if a person, a political party, an army or a school is not attacked by the enemy, for in that case it would definitely mean that we have sunk to the level of the enemy.

LONG-WINDED LADY: That is the last I have in mind.

CHAIRMAN MAO: It is good if we are attacked by the enemy, since it proves that we have drawn a clear line of demarcation between the enemy and ourselves.

LONG-WINDED LADY: And the only desperate conflict is between what we long to remember and what we need to forget. No; that is not what I meant at all. Or ... well, yes, it may *be*; it may be on the nose.

OLD WOMAN: Strange, another thing: when our boys an'
girls was grown,
And when, exceptin' Charley, they'd left us there alone;
When John he nearer an' nearer come, an' dearer seemed
to be,
The Lord of Hosts he come one day an' took him away
from me!

LONG-WINDED LADY: But, wouldn't you think a death
would relate to a life? . . . if not resemble it, *benefit* from
it? Be *taught*? In *some* way? *I* would think.

OLD WOMAN: The Lord of Hosts he come one day an'
took him away from me!

CHAIRMAN MAO: Whoever sides with the revolutionary
people is a revolutionary. Whoever sides with imperialism, feudalism and bureaucrat-capitalism is a counter-
revolutionary.

LONG-WINDED LADY: Be *taught*? In *some* way?

CHAIRMAN MAO: Whoever sides with the revolutionary
people in words only but acts otherwise is a revolutionary
in speech.

LONG-WINDED LADY: *I* would think.

CHAIRMAN MAO: Whoever sides with the revolutionary
people in deed as well as in word is a revolutionary in the
full sense.

VOICE, FROM BOX: And if you go back to a partita . . .
ahhh, what when it makes you cry!?

LONG-WINDED LADY: Savage how it can come, but,
even more the preparations for it. No, not *for* it, but the –
yes! they *must* be preparations for it, unless we're a
morbid species – that, over the duck one day – the cold
duck, with the gherkins and the lemon slices, notched
like a cog . . . and the potato salad, warm if you're lucky,
somebody suddenly says to your husband, when were
you first aware of death, and he's only forty! God!, and
he looks, and he says, without even that flick, that instant

of an eye to me, odd you should ask me and I'm not even
... well, I'm thirty-nine, and I've begun, though if you'd
asked me two weeks ago, though you wouldn't have, and
we saw you then – and it was true; we had; two weeks
ago; two weeks *before*. Is it something that suddenly shows
and happens at once? At one moment? When we are
aware of it we *show* we are? My God!, he said; I hadn't
thought of dying since I was twelve, and, then again,
what, sixteen, *what*, when I wrote those sonnets, all on the
boatman, ironic, though. No! And the other man said,
no: death, not dying.

VOICE, FROM BOX: And if you go back to a partita ...
ahhhh, what when it makes you cry!? Not from the
beauty of it, but from solely that you cry from loss ... so
precious.

OLD WOMAN: Still I was bound to struggle, an' never to
cringe or fall –
Still I worked for Charley, for Charley was now my all;
And Charley was pretty good to me, with scarce a word
or frown,
Till at last he went a-courtin', and brought a wife from
town.

LONG-WINDED LADY: And another man there – an older
man – someone my family had known, some man we had
at parties and once I'd called Uncle, though he wasn't,
some man I think my sister had been seen to go around
with ... someone who was around, said, God, you're
young! You think of death when you're knee-high to a
knicker, and dying when your cock gets decent for the
first or second time, and I mean *in* something, not the
handy-pan, but when you think of *dead*! And ... he was
drunk, though ... what! – well, my lovely husband
looked at him with a kind of glass, and he was a host
then, and he said, with a quiet and staid that I think is –
well, what I have loved him for, or what is of the

substance of what I have loved him for . . . Straight In The Eye! When I was young I thought of death; and then, when I was older – or what I suddenly seemed to be . . . dying . . . with a kind of longing: Ngggggg, with a look at me, as if he could go on . . . and by God!, he slapped away, and it was the first?, the only gesture I was . . . have, been . . . even . . . momentarily . . . DON'T TALK LIKE THAT!!

[*Pause.*]

Slapped away with his eyes and said, I am suddenly dying, to which he added an it would seem, and while everybody tried to talk about death he wanted to talk about dying.

CHAIRMAN MAO: We should support whatever the enemy opposes and oppose whatever the enemy supports.

VOICE, FROM BOX: When art begins to hurt . . . when art begins to hurt, it's time to look around. Yes it is.

LONG-WINDED LADY: But, of course, my sister's . . . saviour, or whatever you would have it, wouldn't not be still. *He* went *on!* Death!, he said. And then he would lapse . . . for nothing, that I could see, beyond the curious pleasure of lapsing . . . Death! Yes, my husband would say, or *said* . . . *said* this particular time – and Bishop Berkeley will be wrong, he added, and no one understood, which is hardly surprising – I am suddenly dying, and I want no nonsense about it! Death? You stop about death, finally, seriously, when you're on to *dying*. Oh, come on!, the other said; death is the whole thing. He drank, as . . . my sister did, too; she died. I think they got in bed together – took a bottle with them, made love perhaps. CRAP! – which quieted the room some . . . and me, too. He never did that. Death is nothing; there . . . there *is* no death. There is only life and dying.

CHAIRMAN MAO: A revolution is not a dinner party, or writing an essay, or painting a picture, or doing embroidery; it cannot be so refined, so leisurely and gentle, so temperate, kind, courteous, restrained and magnanimous. A revolution is an insurrection, an act of violence by which one class overthrows another.

VOICE, FROM BOX: When art begins to hurt, it's time to look around. Yes it is.

LONG-WINDED LADY: And *I*, he said, *I* – thumping his chest with the flat of his hand, slow, four, five times – *I* . . . am *dying*.

CHAIRMAN MAO: After the enemies with guns have been wiped out, there will still be enemies without guns; they are bound to struggle desperately against us, and we must never regard these enemies lightly. If we do not now raise and understand the problem in this way, we shall commit the gravest mistakes.

VOICE, FROM BOX: Yes it is.

LONG-WINDED LADY: And I, he said, I am dying. And this was long before he did. That night he told me: I was not aware of it before. We were resting . . . *before* sex – which we would not have that night; on our sides, his chest and groin against my back and buttocks, his hand between my breasts, the sand of his chin nice against my neck. I always knew I would die – I'm not a fool, but I had no sense of time; I didn't know it would be so soon. I turned; I cupped my hands around his lovely scrotum and our breaths were together. But, it won't be for so very *long*. Yes, he said; I know. Silence, then added; but always shorter.

OLD WOMAN: And Charley was pretty good to me, with scarce a word or frown,

Till at last he went a-courtin', and brought a wife from town.

She was somewhat dressy, an' hadn't a pleasant smile.

CHAIRMAN MAO: People all over the world are now discussing whether or not a third world war will break out.

On this question, too, we must be mentally prepared and do some analysis. We stand firmly for peace and against war. But if the imperialists insist on unleashing another war, we should not be afraid of it.

LONG-WINDED LADY: And I, he said, I am dying.

CHAIRMAN MAO: If the imperialists insist on launching a third world war, the whole structure of imperialism will utterly collapse.

LONG-WINDED LADY: But what about *me*! Think about *me*!

OLD WOMAN: She was somewhat dressy, an' hadn't a pleasant smile –
She was quite conceity, and carried a heap o' style;
But if ever I tried to be friends, I did with her, I know;
But she was hard and proud, an' I couldn't make it go.

LONG-WINDED LADY: ME! WHAT ABOUT ME!

[*Pause.*]

That may give the impression of selfishness, but that is not how I intended it, nor how it is ... at all. *I* ... am *left*. [*Helpless shrug.*] He isn't. I'll not touch his dying again. It was long, and coarse, and ugly, and cruel, and tested the man beyond his ... beyond *anyone*'s capacities. I dare you! I dare anyone! Don't scream! Don't hate! I dare anyone. [*Softer.*] All that can be done is turn into a beast; the dumb thing's agony is none the less, but it doesn't understand *why*, the agony. And maybe that's enough comfort: not to know why.

[*Pause; wistful; sad.*]

But *I* am *left*.

VOICE, FROM BOX: And the beauty of art is order.

CHAIRMAN MAO: We desire peace. However, if imperialism insists on fighting a war, we will have no alternative but to take the firm resolution to fight to the finish before going ahead with our construction. If you are afraid of war day in day out, what will you do if war eventually comes? First I said that the East Wind is prevailing over the West Wind and war will not break out, and now I have added these explanations about the situation in case war should break out. Both possibilities have thus been taken into account.

OLD WOMAN: She was somewhat dressy, an' hadn't a pleasant smile –
She was quite conceity, an' carried a heap o' style;
But if ever I tried to be friends, I did with her, I know.

LONG-WINDED LADY: Besides, his dying is all over; all gone, but his *death* stays. He said death was not a concern, but he meant his own, and for *him*. No, well, he was right: *he* only had his dying. I have both. [*Sad chuckle.*] Oh, what a treasurehouse! I can exclude his dying; I can *not* think about it, except the times I want it back – the times I want, for myself, something less general than ... tristesse. Though that is usually enough. And what for my daughter – *mine*, now, you'll notice; no longer ours; what box have I got for her? Oh ... the ephemera: jewelry, clothes, chairs ... and the money: enough. Nothing solid, except my dying, my death, those two, and the thought of her own. The former, though.

VOICE, FROM BOX: Not what is familiar, necessarily, but order.

CHAIRMAN MAO: War is the highest form of struggle for resolving contradictions, when they have developed to a certain stage, between classes, nations, states, or political groups, and it has existed ever since the emergence of private property and of classes.

LONG-WINDED LADY [*a little stentorian; disapproving*]: Where were *you* those six last months, the time I did *not* need you, with my hands full of less each day; my arms. [*Sad, almost humorous truth.*] If you send them away to save them from it, you resent their going and *they* want what they've missed. Well ... I see as much of you as I'd like, my dear. Not as much as either of us should want, but as much as we do. Odd.

VOICE, FROM BOX: ... and the beauty of art is order – not what is familiar, necessarily, but order ... on its own terms.

OLD WOMAN: But she was hard and proud, an' I couldn't make it go.

She had an edication, an' that was good for her;

But when she twitted me on mine, 'twas carryin' things too fur;

An' I told her once, 'fore company (an' it almost made her sick),

That I never swallowed a grammar, or 'et a 'rithmetic.

LONG-WINDED LADY [*new subject*]: And there I was! Falling!

CHAIRMAN MAO: Revolutionary war is an antitoxin which not only eliminates the enemy's poison but also purges us of our own filth.

VOICE, FROM BOX: That is the thing about music. That is why we cannot listen any more.

[*Pause.*]

Because we cry.

LONG-WINDED LADY: We see each other less, she and I – my daughter – as I said, and most often on boats: something about the air; the burning. She was with me when I fell. Well: on *board*. When they ... hauled me in – oh, what a spectacle *that* was! – there she was, looking on. Not near where I came in, exactly, but some way off: nearer where I'd done it; where it had been done. Red hair flying – not natural, a kind of purple to it, but stunning; quite stunning – cigarette; *always*; the French one. Nails the colour of blood – artery blood, darker than the vein. The things one knows! Looking on, not quite a smile, not quite not. I looked up, dolphins resting on my belly, seaweed-twined, like what's-his-

name, or hers ... I'll bet all you'll say is Honestly,
Mother!

[*Slight pause.*]

And when she came to my cabin, after the doctor, and
the welcome brandy, and the sedative, the unnecessary
sedative ... there she stood for a moment, cigarette
still on, in her mouth, I think. She looked for a moment.
Honestly, Mother!, she said, laughing a little in her
throat, *at* it, humour *at* it. Honestly, Mother! And then
off she went.

VOICE, FROM BOX: That is why we cannot listen any
more.

OLD WOMAN: So 'twas only a few days before the thing
was done –

They was a family of themselves, and I another one;

And a very little cottage one family will do,

But I never have seen a house that was big enough for two.

VOICE, FROM BOX: Because we cry.

LONG-WINDED LADY: Where is she now. This trip.
Mexico. You'd better chain yourself to the chair, she
said to me, later, the day after. You *will* go on deck; put
a long cord on yourself. It's not a usual occurrence, I
told her; not even for me. No, but you're inventive, she
said.

VOICE, FROM BOX: Look! More birds! Another ... sky
of them.

CHAIRMAN MAO: History shows that wars are divided
into two kinds, just and unjust. We Communists oppose
all unjust wars that impede progress, but we do not
oppose progressive, just wars. Not only do we Communists not oppose just wars, we actively participate in them.
All wars that are progressive are just, and all wars that
impede progress are unjust. The way to oppose a war of
this kind is to do everything possible to prevent it before
it breaks out and, once it breaks out, to oppose war with

war, to oppose unjust war with just war, whenever possible.

OLD WOMAN: But I never have seen a house that was big enough for two.

LONG-WINDED LADY: Mexico; still; probably. I'm in Mexico, in case you care, she said. Four A.M. First words, no hello, Mother, or sorry to wake you up if you're sleeping, if you're not lying there, face all smeared, hair in your net, bed jacket still on, propped up, lights out, wondering whether you're asleep or not. No; not that. Not even that. I'm in Mexico, in case you care.

VOICE, FROM BOX: Look! More birds! Another ... sky of them.

LONG-WINDED LADY: Oh. Well ... how very nice. I'm in Mexico, in case you care. I'm with two boys. Sort of defiant. Oh? Well, how nice. Add 'em up and they're just my age; one's twenty and the other's not quite that. Still defiant. Well, that's ... she lies a bit; she's forty-two. That's very *nice*, dear. They're both Mexican. She sounded almost ugly, over the phone, in the dark. Well ... They're both uncircumcised, she said, and then waited. When this happens ... when this happens, she will wait – not those very words, but something she hopes to affect me with, hurt me, shock, perhaps, make me feel less ... well, I was going to say happy, but I am seldom that: not any more ... make me feel less even. She'll wait, and I can hear her waiting, to see if I put the phone down. If I do *not*, after a certain time, of the silence, then she *will*. I put it down gently, when I do. She slams. This time, *I* put it down; gently. I've never known which makes her happier ... if either does, though I suppose one must. Whether she is happier if she makes me do it, or if I pause too long, and she can. I would like to ask her, but it is not the sort of question one can ask a forty-two-year-old woman ... daughter or no.

VOICE, FROM BOX: It's only when you can't come back; when you get in some distant key; that when you say, the tonic! the tonic! and they say, what is *that*? It's *then*.

OLD WOMAN: An' I never could speak to suit her, never could please her eye,

An' it made me independent, an' then I didn't try;

But I was terribly staggered, an' felt it like a blow,

When Charley turned ag'in me, an' told me I could go!

LONG-WINDED LADY: I *do wish* sometimes ... just in general, I mean ... I *do wish* sometimes ...

CHAIRMAN MAO: Some people ridicule us as advocates of the 'omnipotence of war'. Yes, we are advocates of the omnipotence of revolutionary war; that is good, not bad, it is Marxist.

LONG-WINDED LADY: Just in general, I mean ... I *do wish* sometimes ...

CHAIRMAN MAO: Experience in the class struggle in the era of imperialism teaches us that it is only by the power of the gun that the working class and the labouring masses can defeat the armed bourgeoisie and landlords; in this sense we may say that only with guns can the whole world be transformed.

LONG-WINDED LADY: I suppose that's why I came this time ... the Mexicans; the boys. Put an ocean between. It's not as far as a death, but ... still.

OLD WOMAN: 'Over the Hill to the Poor-House,' by Will Carleton.

LONG-WINDED LADY: I remember, I walked to the thing, the railing. To look over. Why, I don't *know*: water never changes, the Atlantic, *this* latitude. But if you've been sitting in a chair, that is what you *do*: you put down the Trollope or James or sometimes Hardy, throw off the rug, and, slightly unsteady from suddenly up from horizontal ... you walk to the thing ... the railing. It's that simple. You look for a bit, smell, sniff, really; you look down to make sure it's moving, and then you think shall you take a turn, and you usually do not; you go back to your rug and your book. Or *not* to your book, but to your *rug*, which you pull up like covers and pretend to go to sleep. The one thing you do *not* do is fall off the ship!

VOICE, FROM BOX: There! More! A thousand, and one below them, moving fast in the opposite way!

OLD WOMAN: I went to live with Susan: but Susan's house was small,
And she was always a-hintin' how snug it was for us all;
And what with her husband's sisters, and what with child'rn three,
'Twas easy to discover that there wasn't room for me.

LONG-WINDED LADY: *Here's* a curious thing! Whenever I'm in an aeroplane – which I am not, often, for I like to choose my company: not that I'm a snob, heavens!, it's my daughter who will not see *me*, or, rather, not often. Not that I am a snob, but I feel that travel in rooms is so much nicer: boats and trains, where one can get away and then out again; people are nicer when you come upon them around corners, or opening doors. But whenever I'm up there, closed in, strapped to my seat, with all the people around, and the double windows, those tiny windows, and the great heavy door, bolted from the outside, probably, even when I'm plumped down in an inside seat – or aisle, as they call them – then! It's then that I feel that I'm going to fall out. Fall right out of the aeroplane! I don't know how I could possibly do it – even through the most ... reprehensible carelessness. I probably couldn't, even if I felt I had to. But I'm sure I will! Always! Though, naturally, I never do.

VOICE, FROM BOX: What was it used to frighten me?

CHAIRMAN MAO: Revolutions and revolutionary wars are inevitable in class society, and without them it is impossible to accomplish any leap in social development and to overthrow the reactionary ruling classes and therefore impossible for the people to win political power.

OLD WOMAN: 'Twas easy to discover that there wasn't room for me.

LONG-WINDED LADY: Coarse, and ugly, and long, and cruel. That dying. My lovely husband.

[*Small pause.*]

But I said I wouldn't dwell on that.

OLD WOMAN: An' then I went to Thomas, the oldest son I've got:

For Thomas's buildings'd cover the half of an acre lot;

But all the child'rn was on me – I couldn't stand their sauce –

And Thomas said I needn't think I was comin' there to boss.

LONG-WINDED LADY: Well! What can we say of an age-ing lady walks bright as you please from her rug and her Trollope or her James or sometimes her Hardy right up to the thing ... the railing; walks right up, puts her fingers, rings and all, right on the varnished wood, sniffs ... that air!, feels the railing, hard as wood, knows it's there – it *is* there – and suddenly, as sudden and sure as what you've always known and never quite admitted to yourself, it is *not* there; there is no railing, no wood, no metal, no buoy-life-thing saying S.S. or H.M.S. whatever, no ... nothing! Nothing at all! The fingers are claws, and the varnish they rubbed against is air? And suddenly one is ... well, what would you expect?! One is suddenly leaning on one's imagination – which is poor support, let me tell you ... at least in *my* case – leaning on that, which doesn't last for long, and over one goes!

VOICE, FROM BOX: ... a thousand miles from the sea. Land-locked, never been, and yet the sea sounds ...

CHAIRMAN MAO: War, this monster of mutual slaughter

among men, will be finally eliminated by the progress of human society, and in the not too distant future, too.

VOICE, FROM BOX: A thousand miles from the sea. Landlocked.

CHAIRMAN MAO: But there is only one way to eliminate it and that is to oppose war with war, to oppose counter-revolutionary war with revolutionary war, to oppose national counter-revolutionary war with national revolutionary war, and to oppose counter-revolutionary class war with revolutionary class war.

VOICE, FROM BOX: Never been, and yet the sea sounds.

CHAIRMAN MAO: When human society advances to the point where classes and states are eliminated, there will be no more wars, counter-revolutionary or revolutionary, unjust or just. That will be the era of perpetual peace for mankind.

OLD WOMAN: But all the child'rn was on me – I couldn't stand their sauce –
And Thomas said I needn't think I was comin' there to boss.

LONG-WINDED LADY: Over one goes, and it's a long way, let me tell you! No falling *up*; no, siree, or out! Straight down! As straight as anything! Plummet! Plut! Well, plummet for sure, plut conjectural. I wonder why I didn't kill myself. Exactly what my daughter said: I wonder why you didn't kill yourself. Though her reading was special. Had a note of derision to it.

OLD WOMAN: An' then I wrote to Rebecca, my girl who lives out West,
And to Isaac, not far from her – some twenty miles at best;
And one of 'em said 'twas too warm there for anyone so old,
And t'other had an opinion the climate was too cold.

VOICE, FROM BOX: Well, we give up something for something.

LONG-WINDED LADY: I did *not* kill myself, as *I* see it, through a trick of the wind, or chance, or because I am bottom heavy. Straight down like a drop of shot! Except. Except, at the very end, a sort of curving, a kind of arc, which sent me gently into a rising wave, or throw-off from the boat, angling into it just properly, sliding in so that it felt like falling on leaves – the pile of autumn leaves we would make, or our brother would, and jump on, like a feather bed. A gust of wind must have done that. Well . . . something did.

CHAIRMAN MAO: 'War is the continuation of politics.' In this sense war is politics and war itself is a political action; since ancient times there has never been a war that did not have a political character. 'War is the continuation of politics by other means.'

VOICE, FROM BOX: Something for something.

CHAIRMAN MAO: It can therefore be said that politics is war without bloodshed while war is politics with bloodshed.

VOICE, FROM BOX: When art hurts. That is what to remember.

LONG-WINDED LADY: I try to recall if I recall the falling, but I'm never sure, I think I do, and then I think I have not. It was so like being awake and asleep . . . at the same time. But I *do* recall being in the water. Heavens! What a sight! *I* must have been, too, but I mean what I *saw*: the sliding by of the ship, green foam in the mouth – kind of exciting – green foam as the wake went by. Lucky you missed the propellers, they said afterwards. Well, yes; lucky.

CHAIRMAN MAO: Without armed struggle neither the proletariat, nor the people, nor the Communist Party would have any standing at all in China and it would be impossible for the revolution to triumph.

OLD WOMAN: And one of 'em said 'twas too warm there for anyone so old,
And t'other had an opinion the climate was too cold.

LONG-WINDED LADY: And sitting there! Sitting there in the water, bouncing around like a carton, screaming a little, not to call attention or anything like that, but because of the fright, and the surprise, and the cold, I suppose; and ... well ... because it was all sort of thrilling: watching the boat move off. My goodness, boats move fast! Something you don't notice till you're off one.

VOICE, FROM BOX: Then the corruption is complete.

OLD WOMAN: So they have shirked and slighted me, an' shifted me about –
So they have wellnigh soured me, an' wore my old heart out;
But still I've borne up pretty well, an' wasn't much put down,
Till Charley went to the poor-master, an' put me on the town.

LONG-WINDED LADY: And then ... and then horns, and tooting, and all sorts of commotion and people running around and pointing ... [*some disappointment*] and then the boats out, the launches, and dragging me in and hauling me up – in front of all those people! – and then the brandy and the nurse and the sedative ... and all the rest.

   [*Pause.*]

I lost my cashmere sweater ... and one shoe.

CHAIRMAN MAO: We are advocates of the abolition of war; we do not want war; but war can only be abolished through war, and in order to get rid of the gun it is necessary to take up the gun.

LONG-WINDED LADY: You're a very lucky woman, I remember the chief purser saying to me, the next day;

I was still groggy. You're a very lucky woman. Yes, I am, I said; yes; I am.

CHAIRMAN MAO: Every Communist must grasp the truth, 'Political power grows out of the barrel of a gun.'

VOICE, FROM BOX: Nothing belongs.

OLD WOMAN: But still I've borne up pretty well, an' wasn't much put down,

Till Charley went to the poor-master, an' put me on the town.

LONG-WINDED LADY: Then, of course, there were the questions. People don't fall off of ocean liners very often. No, I don't suppose they do. Broad daylight and all, people on deck. No; no; I don't imagine so. Do you think you slipped? Surely not! Dry as paint. Have you . . . do you cross often? Oh, heavens, yes! I've done it for years. Have you . . . has this sort of thing ever happened before? What do you take me for!? I'm lucky I'm back from this one, I suppose. Then – gratuitously, and a little peevish, I'm afraid – and I shall cross many times more! And I have – many times, and it's not happened again. Well, do you . . . do you think maybe you were – wincing some here: them; not me – you were helped? Helped? What do you mean? Well . . . aided. What do you mean, *pushed*? Bedside nod. Yes. A laugh from me; a young-girl laugh: hand to my throat, head back. Pushed! Good gracious, no! I had been *reading*. What were you reading – which struck me as beside the point and rather touching. Trollope, I said, which wasn't true, for that had been the day before, but I said it anyway.

[*Some wonder.*]

They didn't know who Trollope was. Well, *there's* a life for you!

OLD WOMAN: Over the hill to the poor-house – my child'rn dear, good-by!

Many a night I've watched you when only God was nigh;

And God'll judge between us; but I will al'ays pray
That you shall never suffer the half I do today.

VOICE, FROM BOX: Look; more of them; a black net . . .
skimming.

[*Pause.*]

And just one . . . moving beneath . . . in the opposite
way.

LONG-WINDED LADY: Isn't that *some*thing? You lead a
whole life; you write books, or you do not; you strive to
do good, and succeed, sometimes, amongst the bad – the
bad never through design, but through error, or chance,
or lack of a chemical somewhere, in the head, or coward-
ice, maybe – you raise a family and live with people, see
them *through* it; you write books, or you do not, and you
say your name is Trollope . . . or whatever it may be, no
matter what, you say your name . . . and they have . . .
never . . . heard of it. That *is* a life for you.

VOICE, FROM BOX: Milk.

CHAIRMAN MAO: People of the world, unite and defeat
the U.S. aggressors and all their running dogs! People
of the world, be courageous, dare to fight, defy difficulties
and advance wave upon wave. Then the whole world will
belong to the people. Monsters of all kinds shall be
destroyed.

OLD WOMAN: 'Over the Hill to the Poor-House,' by Will
Carleton.

VOICE, FROM BOX: Milk.

LONG-WINDED LADY: Is there any chance, do you think
. . . Hm? . . . I say, is there any chance, do you think,
well, I don't know how to put it . . . do you think . . . do
you think you may have done it on purpose? Some
silence. I look at them, my grey eyes gently wide, misting
a little in the edges, all innocence and hurt: *true* innocence;
true hurt. That I may have done it on purpose? Yes;
thrown yourself off. [*Some bewilderment and hurt.*] . . . Me?

CHAIRMAN MAO: People of the world, unite and defeat the U.S. aggressors and all their running dogs.

LONG-WINDED LADY: Well; yes; I'm sorry. Thrown myself off? A clearing of the throat. Yes. Tried to kill yourself. [*A sad little half-laugh.*] Good heavens, no; *I* have nothing to die for.

BOX

Reprise

Perhaps keep the figures from Quotations from Chairman Mao Tse-tung *still and put them in silhouette. Raise the light on the outline of the Box again.*

VOICE:

If only they had *told* us! Clearly! When it was clear that we were not only corrupt – for there is nothing that is not, or little – but corrupt to the selfishness, to the corruption that we should die to keep it ... go under rather than ...

[*Three-second silence. Sigh.*]

Oh, my.

[*Five-second silence.*]

And if you go back to a partita ... ahhhhh, what when it makes you cry!? Not from the beauty of it, but from solely that you cry from loss ... so precious. When art begins to hurt ... when art begins to hurt, it's time to look around. Yes it is.

[*Three-second silence.*]

Yes it is.

[*Three-second silence.*]

No longer just great beauty which takes you more to everything, but a reminder! And not of what *can* ... but what *has*. Yes, when art hurts ...

[*Three-second silence.*]

Box.

[*Two-second silence.*]

So much ... flies. A billion birds at once, black net skimming the ocean, or the Monarchs that time, that island, blown by the wind, but going straight ... in a direction. Order!

[*Two-second silence.*]

When the beauty of it reminds us of *loss*. Instead of the attainable. When it tells us what we cannot have ... well, then ... it no longer relates ... *does* it. That is the thing about music. That is why we cannot listen any more.

[*Pause.*]

Because we cry.

[*Five-second silence.*]

Look! More birds! Another ... sky of them.

[*Five-second silence.*]

What was it used to frighten me? Bell buoys and sea gulls; the *sound* of them, at night, in a fog, when I was very young.

[*A little laugh.*]

Before I had ever seen them, before I had heard them.

[*Some wonder.*]

But I knew what they *were* ... a thousand miles from the sea. Land-locked, never been, and yet the sea sounds ...

[*Three-second silence.*]

But it *couldn't* have been fog, not the sea-fog. Not way back *there*. It was the memory of it, to be seen and proved later. And more! and more! they're all moving! The memory of what we have not known. And so it is with the fog, which I had never seen, yet knew it. And the resolution of a chord; no difference.

[*Three-second silence.*]

And even that can happen here, I guess. But unprovable. Ahhhhh. That makes the difference, does it *not*. Nothing can seep here except the memory of what I'll not prove.

[*Two-second silence. Sigh.*]

BOX   175

Well, we give up something for something.

[*Three-second silence.*]

When art hurts. That is what to remember.

[*Two-second silence.*]

What to look for. Then the corruption . . .

[*Three-second silence.*]

Then the corruption is complete.

[*Five-second silence. The sound of bell buoys and sea gulls begins, faintly, growing, but never very loud.*]

Nothing belongs.

[*Three-second silence. Great sadness.*]

Look; more of them; a black net . . . skimming.

[*Pause.*]

And just one . . . moving beneath . . . in the opposite way.

[*Three-second silence. Very sad, supplicating.*]

Box.

[*Silence, except for the sound of bell buoys and sea gulls. Very slow fading of lights to black, sound of bell buoys and sea gulls fading with the light.*]

PENGUIN PLAYS

Edward Albee

WHO'S AFRAID OF VIRGINIA WOOLF?

'Frighteningly well-observed picture of a matrimonial *corrida*, with the scarred and bloody husband at last taking the cow by the horns after a long, liquor-logged evening' – Alan Brien in the *Sunday Telegraph*

'It has established Albee in the world's mind as the proper successor to Tennessee Williams and Arthur Miller' – Bamber Gascoigne in the *Observer Weekend Review*

'Has an intensity, a demoniac misery, a ferocious humour, an ability to rend and tear and crucify to a degree unfamiliar in the English theatre . . . no one can remain indifferent to its power, its resilience of ideas and its range of language' – Harold Hobson in the *Sunday Times Weekend Review*

A DELICATE BALANCE

A Delicate Balance, which was first performed in London at the Aldwych Theatre in January 1969, was awarded the 1967 Pulitzer Prize for drama. Written with a literary distinction which at times verges on poetry, the dialogue encompasses wit, humour, and compassion.

'A brilliant play. It is a further step in the author's progress and is superior to the more sensational *Who's Afraid of Virginia Woolf?* It deserves our close attention. There will be very few new American plays this season to warrant the same' – *Nation*

Not for sale in the U.S.A. or Canada